Treadwell Walden

Our English Bible and Its Ancestors

Treadwell Walden

Our English Bible and Its Ancestors

ISBN/EAN: 9783337096144

Printed in Europe, USA, Canada, Australia, Japan

Cover: Foto ©Lupo / pixelio.de

More available books at **www.hansebooks.com**

OUR
ENGLISH BIBLE
AND ITS
ANCESTORS.

BY

TREADWELL WALDEN,

RECTOR OF ST. PAUL'S CATHEDRAL, INDIANAPOLIS.

PHILADELPHIA:
PORTER AND COATES,
822 Chestnut Street.

Entered, according to Act of Congress, in the year 1871, by
PORTER & COATES,
in the Office of the Librarian of Congress, at Washington.

MEARS & DUSENBERY, STEREOTYPERS.   H. B. ASHMEAD, PRINTER.

To

The Congregation

of

St. Paul's Cathedral, Indianapolis,

This Account of the Origin and Growth

of

the English Bible,

—already given to them in the form of Lectures—

is

Affectionately Dedicated.

PREFACE.

THE design of this little volume is to give a descriptive narrative of the long and remarkable struggle of the Bible into English—through policies of state, through dogmas of the church, through crudities of public opinion and through changes in the language—with a view: First, to suggest a greater reverence than ever for a work so wisely and heroically produced, and second, to prepare the ordinary reader to form an intelligent idea of the movement toward a more perfect and readable

Bible, which has already begun, and which is certain, if that movement retains the impetus of its history, not to stop until its end be accomplished.

The full account, external and internal, of the English Bible has never yet been written, and all the numerous works which have been composed on the subject, are only contributions to it, but when exhaustively executed it will prove to be a wonderous and fascinating story, not alone to scholars and divines, but to any mind which is aware of the exquisite delicacy of language in itself as a material to be wrought up, of the growth and development of the peculiar English of the Bible, and is quick to see the changes on its surface made by the passing clouds of the century in which it rose into being.

This brief narrative, drawn from many of these sources, it is hoped may give the reader a vivid general impression of the singular evolution of Bible out of Bible until the present noble Version was achieved.

As these pages were written and delivered first in the form of parochial lectures, any redundant picturesqueness of illustration will be sufficiently accounted for by that fact, and doubtless pardoned.

T. W.

St. Paul's Cathedral,
    Indianapolis, May 1871.

CONTENTS.

INTRODUCTION.

The proposed New Revision of the Bible. A movement like that in King James's time. The power and beauty of the present Version. With many the Version supersedes the Originals. Conventional and literary admiration of it. The original purpose and idea of the Version. A diversity of translations thought to be no injury to the popular faith. The best argument for its revision would be a review of its history . . . . Page 9–17

I. THE AGE OF MANUSCRIPT.

THE BIBLE FOR THE PEOPLE.—EARLY SAXON VERSIONS.—THE VERSION OF JOHN WYCLIFFE.—ITS REVISION BY JOHN PURVEY.

Books in manuscript. The Bible doubly locked up. The Greek and Latin Churches prohibiting translations. The English Bible wrought into the history of the English Reformation. Tendency of the English Church to encourage translations. Early Saxon and Norman Version. Only read by the educated among the people. The century before Wycliffe. The rise of the English tongue. Oxford and Cambridge Universities. Wycliffe like Luther. Modes of publication in Wycliffe's day. Chaucer and Mandeville. The effect of his Version. Failure of official attempts to suppress it. Its revision by Purvey. Greek and Hebrew as yet unknown. The Version from the Latin. But the style adopted by Wycliffe since retained in every other Version. The first express endeavor to give the Scriptures to the people. The Version not a progenitor of the present one. Its glory in starting the English and Continental Reformation. The Lollards. Burning of Wycliffe's bones. John Huss and Jerome of Prague, disciples of Wycliffe. Ancient English independence of the Papal Power . . . . . . Page 18–45

II. THE AGE OF PRINTING.

THE FIRST GREEK TESTAMENT.—ERASMUS.—CARDINAL XIMENES.—THE PATRIARCH-VERSION OF WILLIAM TYNDALE.

The Latin Bible the first printed book. The Revival of Learning. The study of Hebrew and of Greek. Erasmus. Dean Colet. Sir Thomas More. Erasmus at Cambridge. He advocates the translation of the Scriptures for the people. He undertakes the publication of a Greek text of the New Testament. Cardinal Ximenes engages in the same work for the whole Bible. The text of Erasmus issued with the works of St. Jerome. The text of Erasmus the first published. This text the basis of all future editions. The first English Version made from the Greek was by William Tyndale. Henry VIII. Luther's Version of the Bible. Birth and education of Tyndale. His controversies with Church dignitaries. His resolve to translate the Scriptures. The general preparation for the undertaking. He applies to the Bishop of London without success. Retires to the Continent. Issues Matthew and Mark. Forced to flee to Worms. Frightful reports of his work reach England. His stratagem for getting the Version into England. Its opposite reception by the people, and by the authorities. In order to disarm opposition he omits his "notes and comments." His repeated revisions of his Version. He undertakes a Version of the Old Testament. Issues Genesis and Deuteronomy, and finally the whole Pentateuch and Jonah. A great change in England—Henry breaks with the Pope. Anne Boleyn's interposition. An edition preparing by the royal printer. Tyndale betrayed and imprisoned. Cranmer's attempt to issue a new Version. Cromwell's attempt. Coverdale's Version. Tyndale executed. The character of Tyndale. Excellencies and peculiarities of his Version. Its individuality and originality. Its influence on the present Version. The favorable condition of the English language when it was executed. A Version should be a direct impersonal transfer from the original, ... Page 46–96

III. THE SIX LINEAL DESCENDANTS OF TYNDALE'S PATRIARCH-VERSION.

THE BIBLES OF COVERDALE, ROGERS, CROMWELL, CRANMER, GENEVA, AND THE BISHOPS.—THE GREEK TESTAMENTS OF STEPHENS AND BEZA.—THE HEBREW TEXT.

The work of Erasmus and Tyndale incomplete. The Greek Text of Stephens. The Greek Text of Beza. The successors of Tyndale. Tyndale's work on the Old Testament. Cranmer's first attempt to issue the English Bible. Cromwell's first attempt. Coverdale. Coverdale issues the whole Bible. Characteristics of his Version. Utility of a diversity of translations. Coverdale's Bible licensed by the king. Tyndale and Coverdale compared. John Rogers. His Version a revision of Tyndale and Coverdale. Its Success. Rogers's Bible the starting-point of all subsequent revisions. Cromwell's second attempt. Coverdale again. Romanists in Paris interrupt the work. The Great Bible. Cranmer's revision of it. Its use enjoined by the king. The popular delight. Scenes in St. Paul's. Posthumous triumph of Tyndale. Edward VI. Greater freedom to the Bible in any Version. Formation of the Prayer-Book. The prosecution under Mary. The revision of the Bible at Geneva. Its remarkable merit. The product of independent minds. Providential advantages. Characteristics which gave it success. Its Bible Dictionary. An unfortunate novelty. The paragraphs broken into verses. The Apocrypha omitted. Accession of Elizabeth. Return of the Bible to England in the Genevan Version. The release of all the Versions. The greater popularity of the Genevan. No official intolerance, as yet, of many Versions. Liberal policy of Archbishop Parker. His project of a new Version. Its successful issue, but no assumption of finality for it. The rivalry of the Versions, Page 97-145

IV. THE PRESENT BIBLE.

ITS FORMATION.—ITS GENERAL EXCELLENCE.—POINTS OF REVISION AND IMPROVEMENT.

Neither the Genevan Version nor the Bishops' satisfactory. James I. The conflict of the Church party and the Puritan party. The Hampton Court Conference. A new Version proposed. The king favors the undertaking. The plan of it elaborated. Composition of the Companies who were to make the revision. The project looked upon as only a new endeavor. The principles of the new revision. The revision simultaneously commenced in 1607 at London, Oxford, and Cambridge. The process. Published after the labor of four years. How it came to be the "Authorized Version." The strange fate and experience of the Genevan Bible before it went out of use. The final acceptance and permanence of the Authorized Version. The elements of its essential perfection and permanency. The elements of its present imperfection and future improvement. A still corrupt original text. Progress of textual criticism. The effect of this and of time on the English text also. A notable deficiency. The Bible too modern. The need of archæological notes to revive its ancient circumstances. Five points of incompleteness. Seven errors of judgment. The translators' imperfect knowledge of Greek and Hebrew. The movement to revision a demand of the age. The historical argument for revision. No extensive alteration designed. The fiery test of adverse criticism has revealed the truth of the originals. So a thorough and fearless revision will insure the permanency of the work, and unfold its full power to the age. Conclusion, . . . Page 146–195

APPENDIX, ... Page 197

INTRODUCTION.

IN Westminster Abbey, to-day, two Companies of Scholars are gathered, engaged in translating the Scriptures anew into the English tongue,—*translating* in the sense of subjecting every part of the present text to a new examination, and returning the whole to the public, revised and retouched wherever it shall prove an inadequate rendering of the original languages. It is a choice assemblage which have this work in hand: bishops, arch-deans, deans, canons, professors, doctors of divinity, of wide-spread fame in the English Church, and, associated with them, men of equal distinction for piety, learning, and scholarship, who do not conform to the "Establishment."

The proposed New Revision of the Bible.

A movement like that in King James's time. In many respects it is a repetition of the celebrated scene in the time of King James the First, when a chosen company of scholars met and labored together for a number of years in the same great work. In some things the two undertakings differ, but only in elements and circumstances peculiar to their time. In other and essential things they are identical. They are identical in the endeavor to meet exactly the same necessity, and in being, each in its own way, the result of a long period of agitation and discussion. It does not matter whether a King appointed the one company or a Convocation has appointed the other, the latter is a lineal and natural successor of the former in the progress of the race and of the language, and represents as vividly a Christian need and demand which exists in the days of Victoria, as the other represented the need and demand which existed in the days of James.

The generality of people are hardly prepared for such a statement as this, and the appointment of these companies of revisers has been, doubtless, a matter of surprise and offence to many persons who do not realize the deficiency of their present Bible, and to many scholars, also, who are so wedded to its aged phraseology by habit and affection, as to overlook too willingly its frequent inadequacy in rendering the meaning and force of the original.

The English Bible, in its present form, two hundred and sixty years old in this year of grace, given to the public, when Shakespeare, and Bacon, and Raleigh, and Ben Jonson, and Drayton, and Beaumont and Fletcher were living to read and admire, the richest formation of that great and plastic era of our language, the "bright consummate flower" of saintly labor and scholarly genius, the wonder of literature, coming down with the works of Shakespeare, and, like them, preserving to us the wealth and force of the Saxon tongue—our Mother English in its simplicity and perfect beauty—the picturesque structure of an age now long gone by, already gray

The power and beauty of the present version.

with antiquity, in whose familiar forms of speech the voices of our forefathers and kindred linger, and the inspiration of the Almighty seems to speak as with the majesty of an original utterance—the English Bible has impressed itself with an almost overpowering authority upon the Christian heart of to-day, and is looked upon, in many cases, as if it were the actual production of the ancient scribe, and its pages are read and pondered over as if they contained the ultimate and unalterable expression of Divine truth.

<small>With many the Version supersedes the originals</small> So are we in danger of repeating, in a new form, the old infirmity of idolatry, which was the worship of the symbol instead of the thing symbolized. We are in danger of looking no further than *this* idol, and of forgetting that which it was intended to represent. We offer to a Version what is due only to the original. Instead of reading the Bible "as through a glass darkly," we read it "as face to face."

This was not the tendency of the century

which produced the "Authorized Version," for neither the people to whom it was given, nor the scholars who had been so active in its preparation, looked upon it as a finality. It underwent a close competition for many years, chiefly with one other excellent version, and its translators had all long passed away before that full tide of enthusiasm set in for it, which has been maintained ever since. As usual in such things, a rhetorical habit of eulogy has gathered about it and invested it with an inapproachable yet conventional sanctity. There are those who profoundly venerate it as a perfect work; and there are those who think that they do. There are others who cling to it with a mingled feeling: partly a literary one, as an invaluable standard of the language, and partly a religious one, as a standard expression also of Divine truth, to question the accuracy of which would be sure to disturb the popular faith. *Conventional and literary admiration of it.*

The latter feeling is the only one which, in a matter of so much reli- *The original purpose and idea of the Version.*

gious importance, can properly have serious consideration; for whatever the Bible may have incidentally become to English literature, this was not its essential purpose. It was translated into the English tongue so that the common people might be able to read it for themselves, and it was, besides, as carefully rendered as the mind and scholarship of the age would allow, in order that it might be cited as a generally accurate and standard authority. But no such pretension ever crowned the faithful work, as that *this* was the end, beyond which there was no possibility of improvement, an *ultima thule* in the vernacular; and no such idea was given to the people as that they beheld the brightness of the Divine face without any interposing veil. The language of the "Translators' Preface," exhibits but one anxious endeavor, to present, if possible, an *improvement* on what had gone before. "Truly," it says, "we never thought from the beginning that we should need to make a new translation, nor yet to make of a bad one a good one, but to make a good one better, or out of many good ones one principal good one, not justly to be excepted against: that hath been our endeavor, that our mark."

While the importance of having one standard which should be universally accepted, was the wise occasion of the great undertaking, yet a diversity of translations was not looked upon with that jealousy or misgiving which prevails in some quarters now. It did no harm to the people, and to the popular faith, at that time, to see the English Bible in the act of struggling out of the originals, or to feel that the scholarship of the age had, after all, only done its best to extract the whole that lay in those mysterious sources. A diversity of translations thought to be no injury to the popular faith.

Certainly, then, the most reasonable way of breaking an almost idolatrous delusion now, and of bringing the subject clearly to "a wise and understanding people," would be to withdraw from the misleading sentimentalism of the present The best argument for its revision would be a review of its history.

day (which is always prone to give to that which is old and venerable a factitious value, seldom discriminating between things which, like wine, time improves, and those which, like a vesture, time deteriorates), and retire into the honest daylight of the age in which this great work was begun, continued, and consummated.

There is one unnoticed and unpondered sentence on the title-page of our Bible, which, like a door, opens directly back into the consciousness of the closing years of that long period: "Translated out of the original Tongues, and *with the former translations diligently compared and revised.*" If the modern printers had not left out the word "*newly*" before "translated," which appears in the early copies, we should have had an additional suggestion of recency to carry our minds back into that time.

But when we get there, even so far as the days of King James, we must needs travel still further back, with the ancient fathers of the Authorized Version, into what was a long-past age to them, as difficult for them to realize and restore, as theirs is to us, but in which are to be found the fountains of the great movement of the Bible into English, which in their day had grown into such a mighty stream.

I.

THE AGE OF MANUSCRIPT.

The Bible for the People.—Early Saxon Versions.—The Version of John Wycliffe.—Its Revision by John Purvey.

IT is hard for us, in this day, sitting amid myriads of books, to go behind the Printing Press and to realize the long series of ages when a Book was a rare and curious wonder, and when the ability to read was an accomplishment equally rare and marvellous. And yet it was under just such conditions that the Scriptures were first written, and under the same they remained in every country where they were taken, and in every language into which they were translated, until only four hundred and thirty years ago. One man had to read for a thousand—often for ten

Books in manuscript.

thousand, and much that was written had to go forth on the surface of the people in the transmuted form of oral explanation. The pulpits stood up in an ocean of popular ignorance, dim light-houses of instruction, as well as of guidance, to unreading millions.

The Bible doubly locked up. But, on the other hand, the very mystery which enveloped the Scriptures—scriptures, then, in the most literal sense—as sources of Divine knowledge, in which lay the precious story of the Life of Christ, the history of the Chosen People, and the total Revelation of heavenly truth to man, could not but stimulate the curiosity of the people to be more fully informed about them. And when, in addition to this, they were known to be doubly locked up, first in the ancient, and what had become the ecclesiastical Latin tongue, and next, even as such, jealously kept within the cloisters of the church, the popular eagerness to become acquainted with their contents could hardly have had a greater incitement. We ourselves cannot realize the power of this threefold incentive to curiosity except by putting ourselves into this long-past situation, and imagining our minds in such a darkness as would blot out our present enlightened consciousness of Christianity and our ability to read the Bible in our native tongue, and then, in all that strange obliviousness, to fancy ourselves hearing vaguely of the inspired authorities of our religion as sealed up in another, and not the original, language, and getting all our knowledge of it through the muffled dogmas of a church and the muzzled mouths of its priests! It is all a matter of imagination now, but it was a hungry, anxious reality then; and such is the condition of things amid which this history opens.

So, it will be noticed, in going back into these ages, we come upon a greater obstacle to the diffusion of the Bible than even a general ignorance of letters. We come upon this traditional policy of the Church, which in both its branches, the Greek and the Latin, had from the earliest times "interdicted

<small>The Greek and Latin Churches prohibiting translations.</small>

the translation of the Scriptures into any vernacular tongue." And this policy became only the more intensified and deeply rooted as time went on and education began to spread among the laity, and the symptoms of a disposition to read and think for themselves, grew more strongly manifest.

The English Bible wrought into the history of the English Reformation. The experience of the Bible in its endeavors to reach the people has its best and most heroic history in the case of the Anglo-Saxon mind and of the English tongue. The spirit of Anglican independence of the Roman rule has in this its most striking illustration, and the annals of the Reformation in England are bound up and identical with the annals of the English Bible.

Tendency of the English Church to encourage translations. There would seem to have been a remarkable tendency in the early English Church, before Roman interference set in so strongly, to bring the Scriptures to the common people. In the great British collections, the libraries of Oxford, of Cambridge, and of the British Museum, many vestiges of this tendency may be found in curious fragments of Anglo-Saxon and Anglo-Norman versions: rude and imperfect attempts to get portions of the Bible into the vernacular. *Early Saxon and Norman Versions.* The oldest of these, attributed to Cædmon, a monk, is the Bible history paraphrased in the alliterative verse of Anglo-Saxon poetry. The venerable Bede, who always wrote in Latin, is yet associated with a version of St. John's Gospel in his native tongue. A Psalter is extant, said to be by a Saxon Bishop of the seventh century. A few chapters of Exodus and the Psalms were translated by King Alfred, who is recorded to have said that he desired " all the free-born youth of his kingdom should be able to read the English Scriptures."* There are three versions of the Gospels and some fragments of the Old Testament referred to the ninth and tenth centuries. Three or four more of the Gospels are assigned to the eleventh and twelfth cen-

---

* Plumptre—Smith's Bible Dict. iii. 1665.

turies. Then, in the thirteenth century, a translation into Norman French of the whole Bible by an unknown hand, and various fragmentary versions of the Psalms, and other portions of the Bible, seem to have appeared here and there; all in uncouth, grotesque, and unintelligible lettering to the modern eye —but hungrily read by the educated among the people of those passing centuries.

<small>Only read by the educated among the people.</small> It is doubtful how far these were intended for the masses, as the knowledge of letters had not yet gone down among the lower orders; but it is evident that some of the higher and wealthier classes were familiar with the Scriptures in their native tongue. And so, it would appear, after all, that these Versions must have been shut up in the cloister, the cell, the circles of the court, and the houses of the opulent, mere rush-lights in a densely dark age; and all of them would seem to have burned so far apart, or in such seclusion, not to say oblivion, that when Wycliffe turned to his task of translating the Bible,

he is found complaining that there was nothing extant to help him.*

Though still the age of manuscript, the century before Wycliffe had witnessed a gradual emergence from the gross darkness of these earlier times. It was comparatively an age of thought and of reading among the laity; quite enough to create an immense appreciation of his labors on the part of the people. *(The century before Wycliffe.)*

The mind of all these later centuries had been active enough, and learning had been cultivated to a very great extent, but the thinkers and scholars were mostly to be found in the ranks of the clergy. The learned always wrote in Latin. The nobles spoke in Norman-French. But the people still clung to the Anglo-Saxon of their ancestors, and this was destined to become the noble and enduring basis of that future English tongue which all alike were *(The rise of the English tongue.)*

---

* Plumptre—Smith's Bible Dict. iii. 1665.

in time to employ both in speech and literature. To indicate its long submergence under these other and more customary modes of speech and writing, and its slow ascension into use and power, the fact may be mentioned that not till the middle of the fourteenth century was a legal instrument put into English, and the close of that century drew near before it was recognised and spoken in Parliament.

<small>Oxford and Cambridge Universities.</small> The thirteenth and fourteenth centuries witnessed also another advance. Those great seats of learning, Oxford and Cambridge, which had heretofore been only single and concentrated schools, now became each that collection of colleges which distinguishes them to-day. It was then that those separate institutions were founded, and those venerable structures reared, which now are so antiquated and picturesque, and which, with their scholastic traditions, have come down to us laden with the romantic associations of a forming thought and literature, just as the old castles of Eng-

land linger in the present to be the ancient sanctuaries of its history, and the cathedrals are cherished as the ancient fortresses of its religion.

There are said to have been thirty thousand students in the University of Oxford in the beginning of the fourteenth century :* and this was the century in which John Wycliffe was born, and grew into pre-eminent distinction as a scholar, a theologian, a philosopher, a writer of many controversial tracts, an independent student of the Scriptures, and finally, (with the aid of his friend Nicolas of Hereford in part of the Old Testament), the translator of the whole Bible from the Latin quoted by the schoolmen into the English spoken by the people.

Wycliffe was, in his day and generation, an anticipation of Luther, and almost the same circumstances seemed to have produced him as those which

Wycliffe like Luther.

---

* Illus. Hist. Eng. i. 813.

afterwards produced the great German Reformer. He was a man who had drank deep of the Scriptures, and to whom they had become the only rule of faith and doctrine in opposition to a church which had found it convenient to forget and to conceal those earliest wells of its inspiration and guidance. He stood out against the four powerful religious orders of his time as corrupt and noxious societies. He braved their rage and curses when the preponderating influence of the Church was at their back, and succeeded in lowering somewhat their public repute. He met the Bishops in controversy, and had to endure frequent episcopal persecution. He withstood even the Pope again and again, and was made the object of many Papal bulls. Luther, himself, was not so distinguished in the outset of his career, nor so personally formidable as a scholar and theologian,—"the first casuist in the Empire,"*—and the holder of high preferments in the gift of the Church,

* English Hexapla 7.

nor was he any more alert and bold, in the proportion of his opportunity, in challenging the avalanche of Papal wrath to fall. And, as it afterward turned out in the mind of Luther, so it now turned out in the mind of Wycliffe: an almost immediate determination to assume the extraordinary task of translating the entire Bible into the language of the common people, as the first and best means of acquainting them with the truth, and bringing all the strength of their uprising against the corruptions of the Church.

The merit of undertaking the self-same gigantic labor was all the greater that he had no such means or encouragement as the Printing Press at hand to spread his work by thousands, but was shut up to the simple and sluggish vehicles of publication known to his time.

When any one would publish, in those days, instead of committing his book, as now, to the quickly multiplying types, he gave it to professional copyists, or he

Modes of publication in Wycliffe's day.

himself pronounced it slowly from a pulpit erected in some public place, and there it was taken down by all who desired to possess a transcript. This was the halting way in which it became distributed among the people.* In like manner, doubtless, were the English Scriptures laboriously copied from Wycliffe's own manuscript, and borne into the secret recesses of English homes to be read, or heard read, in gratitude and wonder by the people as their own first fresh communion with the veritable oracles of God.

<small>Chaucer and Mandeville.</small> Chaucer and Mandeville, whose works now mark the dawn of the present English tongue, were contemporaries of Wycliffe, and, as the former has been called the father of English poetry, so Wycliffe now earned a greater right than the latter to be called the father of English prose.

<small>The effect of his Version.</small> The work of translation occupied him many years, and it was the frequent theme of his tracts long before it was

---

* English Hexapla 8.

finished. The version appeared about 1380, and was of course copied eagerly and read everywhere. It was wildly protested against by his opponents, for, like the opening of windows in a long-closed building given up to the owls and the bats, this was opening the windows of a corrupt church which had shut itself up in darkness, "because its deeds were evil," and the pouring in of the whole blaze of God's sunlight to its insupportable disturbance. The swarming friars of the mendicant orders, who were battening on the ignorance and credulity of the people, were stirred from their places by the exposure. The unclean lives of the clergy could not endure the revelation of the pure and spotless life of Christ.* The complaint of Knighton, a church dignitary of the time, gives us an inside view of the priestly discomfiture. "The gospel" (writes he) "which Christ committed to the clergy and doctors of the church, that they might sweetly dispense it to the laity and weaker persons, according

*Westcott. History of the English Bible 19.

to the exigency of the times, and the wants of the people, hungering after it in their mind, this John Wycliffe has translated into the *Anglican,* not *angelic,* language; whence, through him, it has been published and disclosed more openly to laymen and women able to read, than it used to be to the most learned and intelligent of the clergy—and so the gospel pearl is cast abroad, and trodden under foot of swine; and what was dear to clergy and laity is now rendered, as it were, the common jest of both; so that the gem of the church becomes the derision of laymen, and that is now theirs for ever, which before was the special property of the clergy and doctors.*

Yes, it was "now theirs for ever." The great, brave, dangerous, but all necessary movement people-ward had begun, and the response of the people was never afterwards wanting. Wycliffe did not live to see it, but the released glad tidings went everywhere among them, and the new faith flew from mouth

* English Hexapla 7.

to mouth and heart to heart. It is the record of an enemy to the movement that the country was so full of converts that "a man could not meet two people on the road, but one of them was a disciple of Wycliffe." The Londoners were declared to be "nearly all Lollards,"* the name of reproach by which his followers were known.

Among the foremost who were alarmed by the growing reformation was Arundel, Archbishop of Canterbury, who set himself to extinguish its occasion, and procured a decree of Convocation threatening the "greater excommunication" upon any one who should read Wycliffe's version, or any other, in whole or in part, publicly or privately. It is a remarkable indication of how widely, nevertheless, the Bible continued to be copied and secretly read by both rich and poor, that about one hundred and fifty copies of it, and of the revised edition of it by John Purvey, some of them sumptuously illuminated and

_{Failure of official attempts to suppress it.}

---

* Blunt's Dictionary of Theology 429.

bound, are now in existence, which had eluded Arundel's vigilant and destroying search.

<small>Its revision by Purvey.</small> Without a notice of this subsequent revision the account of Wycliffe's work would not be complete. John Purvey, "who boarded with Wycliffe, partook largely of his instructions, and completely imbibed his opinions, continuing his companion to his dying day," about four years after his death undertook the re-issue of his version on a scale of most elaborate and painstaking improvement. Purvey seems to have stood in very much the same relation to Wycliffe, that John Rogers afterwards did to Tyndale, revising the version of Wycliffe in the New Testament, and the version of Nicolas of Hereford in the Old, as Rogers revised Tyndale in the New and Coverdale in the Old.

<small>Greek and Hebrew as yet unknown. The Version from the Latin.</small> But the material with which both the translator and his reviser had to work was very different from that which was at hand a century and a half later. The Greek and Hebrew originals were

not known, and the study of these languages, except in very rare instances, had ceased in Western Europe. Wycliffe, distinguished scholar as he was, remained almost totally ignorant of both. The only form in which the Bible was accessible was in the Latin translation of St. Jerome, made in the fourth century, called the Vulgate. This was all that the Roman Church would recognise, and even this, as we have seen, it interdicted the laity from using. The copies of this Latin version, then in existence, were none of them clear of gross errors in the text. The version of Wycliffe was of course infected with these corruptions, and as soon as it got into wide circulation the necessity of a revision on the basis of a purer text became manifest. The revision was carefully and conscientiously done by Purvey, who also retouched the version throughout, and it is this form of Wycliffe's Bible which finally took hold of the age and which has come down to the present time.

But Purvey did not change the diction which

But the style adopted by Wycliffe since retained in every other Version.

Wycliffe had adopted, and which was purposely neither scholarly nor courtly, but the simple, homely Saxon speech of the people; the style of the Bible in every one of the seven subsequent versions, including that which we accept to-day. In his ideas also of what constituted both spiritually and philologically an especial fitness for the work we doubtless see the spirit and power of his great predecessor, and therefore the more eminent name still justly absorbs the authorship and renown of the wonderful achievement.

The first express endeavor to give the Scriptures to the people.

Few are prepared to realize the extraordinary character of this pioneer attitude of Wycliffe, and especially the greatness of his undertaking not only to translate, for this had been done before, but *to put the Scriptures into circulation among the people.* The boldness of the act, its wisdom and far-sightedness, and the personal willingness in one of his eminence and distinction to stand almost alone in defence of and responsibility for convictions that were then novel and remarkable, cannot be overestimated, especially when we see the great historic result which afterward justified and glorified him.

But, although in the group of English-Bible heroes we count him the foremost, yet in the golden chain of the translations his version cannot be included. It was only a translation of a translation. The time was yet to come when men should render direct from the inspired originals; but,—though by this vital distinction detached, and standing alone, without descent, as it was without ancestry, and as "born out of due time,"—still the immense interest will always invest it of being, after a spiritual and Providential order, in the line of the ancestry of our English scriptures, the first to meet the hunger of the people, the first to kindle the fires of the Reformation, and destined to stand for ever as the earliest beacon light of that appeal to the people, and of that faith in the

The Version not a progenitor of the present one.

wisdom of the popular judgment and will which has since moved over both church and state, and which will finally illumine and regenerate the world.

<small>Its glory in starting the English and Continental Reformation.</small> The New Testament of Wycliffe, even now as a printed book, is far withdrawn from the English apprehension by its antique Saxonisms of style and spelling, and was almost as unreadable to the next generation of reformers as to ourselves; but this is its everlasting glory,—the glory of an extinct luminary—it made itself an epoch, and it gathered around it the first organized and formidable resistance which ever occurred, to Romish corruption both in doctrine and life. The antiquated version will always have this magnificent association. Wycliffe gave it to his followers, and as the Roman Catholic historian, Dr. Lingard, justly says: "In their hands it became an engine of wonderful power. Men were flattered with the appeal to their private judgment; the new doctrines insensibly acquired partisans and protectors in the

higher classes, who alone were acquainted with the use of letters; a spirit of inquiry was generated; and the seeds were sown of that religious revolution, which, in a little more than a century, astonished and convulsed the nations of Europe."

The history of that century when <small>The Lollards.</small> these "seeds" were working in English soil, is a history which belongs to the State as well as to the Church of England. The emancipation of the people took a political as well as a theological direction. The Lollards became a dreaded power; high dignitaries and distinguished names appeared among them. They represented an uncomfortable amount of the intelligence and thought of the people, and sometimes so turbulently that both the Church and the State agreed to imprison, to hang, and to burn. The "Lollards' Tower," often in this day a conspicuous part of the episcopal palaces of England, is a vestige of that early spiritual and political rebellion; now the monument of its history and sufferings, as it was then the prison of its temporary repression.

<small>Burning of Wycliffe's bones.</small> In the midst of it all Wycliffe himself experienced a most singular and typical resurrection. An order came from Pope Martin the Fifth, nearly a half-century after he had fallen dead at the foot of the altar of his parish church at Lutterworth, commanding his bones to be dug up and burned; and the now quick and fiery ashes of those aged bones, already crumbling fast enough by nature into their original dust, were scattered on the Swift, a little streamlet which ran by the churchyard where he lay.

"Thus," says old Fuller, ready both as a poet and a prophet to catch the augury, "this brook hath conveyed his ashes into Avon; Avon into Severn; Severn into the narrow seas; they into the main ocean; and thus the ashes of Wycliffe are the emblem of his doctrine which is now dispersed all the world over." Or, as a more sprightly pen of the same day put it:—

> "The Avon to the Severn runs,
>   The Severn to the Sea,
> And Wycliffe's dust shall spread abroad,
>   Wide as the waters be."

Even so his followers survived every persecution, and when, in the reign of Henry the Eighth, the power of Rome in England was broken and expelled, they were the first to join and swell the tide of that renewed movement toward Reformation which resulted in the complete independence of the English Church, and finally of Protestants of every name who spoke the English tongue.

Wycliffe—while he died a natural death, and only by an accident escaped martyrdom at the stake—that accident being the onset against each other of two rival Popes—was himself the spiritual father of two famous martyrs on the other side of the English Channel. It was owing to him that both John Huss and Jerome of Prague, men of scholarship, eloquence, courage, and an influence which terrified the ecclesiastics of their

John Huss and Jerome of Prague, disciples of Wycliffe.

day, rose up in their place in Bohemia and agitated for the reformation of a corrupt church, nearly a century before Luther was born, and did for the coming religious revolution on the continent what Wycliffe had done for it in England.—"Wycliffe" was their watchword. They publicly proclaimed his writings and their adoption of his doctrines. They made his name ring far and wide through Europe. The church authorities caught up and burned his "pernicious" books—and at last both John Huss and Jerome were also caught up, hurried to the stake and burned: their ashes, thrown upon the swift waters of the Rhine, to go, like Wycliffe's, over the broad sea, as their spirit and power had already gone everywhere over the ocean of the people to make the Reformation under Luther only the grand outburst of a long-brewing storm which should cause that ocean to rage and swell.

But this historic reminiscence of Wycliffe and his work awakens still another association nearer to ourselves.

His Bible is a memorial stone of English independence in sentiment and feeling, of Rome and the Papal Power, one hundred and fifty years and more before Henry the Eighth found it personally and dynastically convenient to drive out that intruding authority, and to be constituted himself the "Head of the Church." The ability of Henry to do this lay not in himself, but in the latent, long-growing and radical alienation of the English people from the Pope. As in primitive Saxon, or rather British times, the days of Gregory and his far-famed missionary to Britain, St. Augustine, an independent church already existed there with its bishops and complete Episcopal organization, so it had continued, in every after-century since, notwithstanding the growth of Roman influence, to exhibit a reserve, manifested in some outbreak, royal or otherwise, until in the person of Wycliffe and his followers it struggled apart in a way that history has been especially called to record. And thus we find in the

Ancient English independence of the Papal Power.

epoch of Wycliffe, not of Luther, on English soil, not German, in the English Church, not the Roman, in the fourteenth century, not the sixteenth, the power and the feeling down among the people which made Henry the Eighth afterward possible as the leader of the English Reformation, and that development possible of organized independence, by which the church resumed her primitive character, and in which she has since proceeded alone.

Just as primitive Christianity, struggling for existence, reached at last in the Emperor Constantine the political and the state opportunity to rise into power and grandeur, so did the primitive English Church, after suffering from this alien intrusion nearly a thousand years, reach in its bold bad monarch a political and a state occasion when it became a separate establishment in its own insular realms.

Thus the sheaf of wheat, which had this rich outburst of golden grain in the time of Henry the Eighth, and which had been cut from the British soil in those early Saxon centuries, found its binding circlet midway, during the reign of Edward the Third, in the ripe movement of Wycliffe, the English Reformer; and so does that great Church still s‘and up, across the sea, a bound historic sheaf, after a long growth and precarious fruitage now safely harvested, old in herself, but young in her grain-seeds; the power which has spread, and is still destined to spread everywhere, the glad tidings of Jesus Christ wherever the English language is spoken and the English Bible read.

II.

THE AGE OF PRINTING.

THE FIRST GREEK TESTAMENT.—ERASMUS.—CARDINAL XIMENES.—THE PATRIARCH VERSION OF WILLIAM TYNDALE.

BETWEEN sixty and seventy years after the death of Wycliffe, in the middle of the fifteenth century, the night of the Dark Ages passed away, and the sun of the new civilization rose in its strength; and, like the natural sun, it found the world prepared for its rising. There was every instinct alive and abroad to greet, and to grow under, the great and sudden illumination. This sun was the Printing Press.

Between the years 1450–55 John Gutenberg, even while he held the precious product of his genius trembling in his hands, fearful of some one discovering and stealing his treasure, printed as his first publication the Latin Bible.* The Bible, then, was the first book from the Press! The dawn of the new Day was even so correspondent to the opening mind of the departing Night. Strange giving again to the people! Inevitable movement of Providence!

<small>The Latin Bible the first printed book.</small>

When the sun rises, it first spreads abroad the diffused glory of the dawn, but when it reaches the horizon line it appears to *rush up* and reveals almost all its disk at once. Nothing can exhibit the instantaneous leap of this new sun, and the sudden outflood of its effulgence upon mankind, more vividly than the simple statistics of that amazing era as it opened. Before the close of the ever memora-

---

* Published in 1452,—a splendid and beautiful volume. Scrivener. "Introduction to the Criticism of the New Testament," 262.

ble fifteenth century, above one thousand printing presses were going in two hundred and twenty places in Europe. One hundred different editions of the Latin Bible had been issued,* and Bibles had been printed in Spanish, Italian, French, Dutch, German, and Bohemian versions.†

The English Bible was not yet forthcoming. It still remained in the manuscripts of the Wycliffites. But, for that matter, all of these Continental translations, like that of Wycliffe, were only secondary translations—versions of the Vulgate.

<small>The Revival of Learning.</small> Meantime, through all this half-century, the press was teeming with many other works, chiefly the Latin and Greek classics, and literature, in all the branches then known, entered upon its new and greater life. The eager study of the Greek and Hebrew languages was the first outburst of this "Revival of Learning."

* Anderson. Annals of English Bible lxiii. Introd.
† Westcott. Hist. Eng. Bib. 30.

The Latin version of the Bible could no longer satisfy the new mind which had come into being. The theological thirst for truth and the religious excitement of the day sent every active intellect far back of this ecclesiastical cistern to the original but long-forgotten wells of the "living" water. It was religious inquiry which led the way to the study and resuscitation of these dead literatures, and when they revived, it was first in the form of the printed Old and New Testaments. The striking declaration of an eminent authority, quoted by Mr. Westcott, is therefore as true as it is picturesque, that "Greece had risen from the grave with the New Testament in her hand."*

But the Hebrew language had risen first in the publication of a text of the Old Testament in 1488, when as yet only a few, except Jews, could read it. The Greek text of the New Testament did not appear for more than a quarter of a century afterwards. It had to wait until the

The study of Hebrew and of Greek.

---

* Westcott. Hist. Eng. Bib. 30.

knowledge of that language had been sufficiently acquired by the scholars of the day. But when it came, it came by way of England. The springs which fed that fountain of scholarship were found in Oxford.

The history of this reads almost like a romance, and it keeps the English Church conspicuously in the line of the splendid succession.

About nine years after the He- <small>Erasmus.</small> brew text had been published, and while the study of Greek was gathering at the great university centres, the illustrious Erasmus, then in his youth, and already famous as a scholar, but prematurely wasted in form and feature with poverty and study, came over from Holland to England in order to perfect his knowledge of the Greek in the University of Oxford. It was there that a remarkable and lovely triple friendship formed between himself, John Colet, afterward the celebrated Dean of St. Paul's, and Thomas More, afterward the equally celebrated Lord Chancellor of the kingdom. The three have since been called the "Oxford Reformers of 1498." In the advanced and bold intelligence of these young and gifted men, and in their frank discussion with each other of the theological questions which were agitating the period, lay the beginning of a subsequent opposition to the dogmatic subtleties and speculations of the "Schoolmen," who were the surviving Pharisees of the Dark Ages just left behind, and who were arrayed in stout phalanx for many years in defence of the church as it was. This became the great controversy of the time. A powerful party in the Roman Church resisted the "New Learning," as the study of Hebrew and Greek was called, and every one who had in him an advanced idea therein was accused of resisting the church. In the heat of the conflict it was declared that the study of Greek would make men Pagans, and that the study of Hebrew would make them Jews! The dear old Latin version was pathetically declared to be crucified between two thieves, and the Greek was the one thief, the Hebrew the other!

In such idolatry as this was held the Latin translation, and in such a strength of prejudice and prepossession stood the mass of empty scholastic speculation and theological dogmatism which had obtained until that time.

Dean Colet. Sir Thomas More. Meantime Erasmus rapidly increased in reputation as the first scholar and philologist in Europe. The old college friendship remained in full force, and the old congeniality of views continued and intensified. Dean Colet, preaching in St. Paul's, grew clearer and stronger in declaring that the study of the Life of Christ and of the Epistles of St. Paul were nearer the heart of Christianity, and more influential in the Christian life, than all the cold and empty dogmas of the schools. But Sir Thomas More, while in continued sympathy with the war upon the schoolmen for the right to the "New Learning," was less pronounced in his opposition to the Church as it was.

Erasmus at Cambridge. In 1509, Erasmus, ripe in Greek and every other knowledge of his

day,—now a great reputation everywhere—
returned to England from a sojourn on the
continent, and took up his abode, not in Oxford, but in the University of Cambridge, as
the Professor of Theology and Greek. His
fame as the champion of an emancipated
scholarship drew around him many whom the
position of the Church on this subject had
alienated. He remained there nearly five
years, and, during that time, his influence in
"awakening the English mind was greater
than that of Luther and Zuinglius." So did
he repay to England, by the liberality of his
genius, the debt he owed to the generosity of
her scholarship. "The credit," says Anderson,* "of being one of the first learned men in
Europe, who argued strongly for learning being
cultivated, with a view to the benefit and instruction of the common people, can never be
taken from Erasmus." What he had demanded for himself, he demanded for every-
one, and the inevitable conclusion of such a

* Annals of the Eng. Bib. i. 24.

mind as his was the right of every one to read the Scriptures; not only the right of the learned to read them in the originals, but the right of those who were not learned to read them in their native tongue. Hear him, in his famous essay, called the "Paraclesis:"* "I utterly dissent from those who are unwilling He advocates the translation of the Scriptures for the people. that the Sacred Scriptures should be read by the unlearned, translated into their vulgar tongue, as though Christ had taught such subtleties that they can scarcely be understood even by a few theologians, or as though the strength of the Christian religion consisted in man's ignorance of it. The mysteries of kings it may be safer to conceal, but Christ wished His mysteries to be published as openly as possible. I wish that even the weakest woman should read the Gospels— should read the Epistles of St. Paul. And I wish they were translated into all languages. * * * To make them understood is surely the first step. * * * I long that the husband-

---

* "Oxford Reformers," 256.

man sing portions of them to himself as he follows the plough, that the weaver should hum them to the time of his shuttle, that the traveller should beguile with their stories the tedium of his journey."

Erasmus, so wise as never to take an extreme position in his life, so evenly balanced as always to resist Romish bigotry on one side, and Protestant radicalism on the other, declared again and again this remarkable and revolutionary conviction, which, while it would seem to question the authority of the former and encourage the tendency of the latter, really made him in his own person the earliest layer of that essential foundation, deeper than which no speculation or controversy could go. *It was Erasmus who became the founder of the New Testament in printed Greek.* It was he who laid the original masonry on which the structure of the next English version was to rise. At the solicitation of Froben, a celebrated printer of Basle, he undertook the

<small>He undertakes the publication of a Greek text of the New Testament.</small>

great work of forming a text out of the few and scanty Greek manuscripts of the New Testament Scriptures, which were then known and accessible, and of publishing it to the world. The wide-spread interest in the enterprise, started under such eminent auspices, may be imagined.

Cardinal Ximenes engages in the same work for the whole Bible. Before it had been begun rumors had come of a similar undertaking contemplated and commenced by the celebrated Cardinal Ximenes, in the University of Alcala, in Spain, to be performed on a splendid scale, with every facility in the employment of many learned men, access to the best manuscripts, and the use of the finest presses. But the poor and single-handed scholar, urged by his printer, worked the more earnestly to anticipate the issue of his formidable competitor. No manuscript earlier than the tenth century was known to him, and, of all he collated, none were perfect enough to furnish him with a complete text. In a few instances he was obliged to supply a chasm in the Greek by rendering back the Latin Vulgate into Greek. A thing, by the way, which Ximenes himself was also obliged to do.*

The venerable Froben gave himself to the work with self-forgetful devotion: like his co-laborer, thoughtful not of pecuniary profit, but of developing an undertaking which was of such importance to the age and to be so fruitful for human good.

But Erasmus had projected the work in a combination which gave both himself and his printer a task of immense magnitude. *(The text of Erasmus issued with the works of St. Jerome.)* He had resolved to bring out simultaneously with the Greek of the New Testament, the works of the great father, Jerome, who himself had, eleven hundred years before, taken a stand in some respects similar to that of the present reformers, and had advocated, amid much opposition, a version of the Greek Scriptures in the Latin vernacular, on the basis of an old Latin version

* See Tregelles. "Account of the Printed Text of the Greek New Testament," 21.

already in existence but very corrupt, and who finally had produced this self-same Vulgate, now so universally received as the standard and ultimate authority!* There was a poetic symmetry, therefore, and something more, in the resolve to print the works of the great author of this early version, with the long-neglected and now disparaged original.

<small>The text of Erasmus the first published.</small> In the race with the Cardinal and his co-laborers, the lone scholar came out first. In fact the Cardinal did not race at all, but kept back his work till he had the whole Bible in print. The year 1516 is memorable for the appearance of the New Testament, for the first time, in print.†

It came out in the heavy, lumbering volumes of the primitive press, and from that moment

---

* "St. Jerome was the father who in his day strove to give to the people the Bible in their vulgar tongue." Oxford Reformers 265.

† Strictly speaking, part of the Cardinal's N. T. was in print before Erasmus's text went to press. But Erasmus's text was the first *published*.

the yellow and aged transcripts on parchment and paper, the heritage and work of monastic copyists for a thousand years or more, entered the era of endless youth, freshness, and standard accuracy.

Accompanying this (in subsequent revisions) was even another evidence of labor and devotion: a new version in Latin by Erasmus and theological notes.

The work, so complete in idea if not in execution, raised, as might have been expected, a storm of opposition and a host of enemies. *This text the basis of all future editions.* Six years afterward the splendid volumes of Cardinal Ximenes appeared. But, by this time, Erasmus had made and published three revisions of his own work. Only six hundred copies, in all, were issued of the Complutensian Polyglot, as Ximenes' work was called. It was therefore very scarce and little used.* In his next revision and edition, the fourth, Erasmus made it contribute to the

---

* Tregelles. "Historical Account of the Printed Greek Text of the New Testament," 27.

perfection of his own text, and so it came to pass that the Greek text of Erasmus, the one first issued and the one most widely circulated, maintained its place as a foundation, which others might improve but not supersede. In the progress of early textual criticism, after this, the work of Ximenes continued to be used by others also, but only as a side contribution to the greater purity of the text, which was still anxiously sought.

The first English Version made from the Greek was by Wm. Tyndale. We now take a step further in our history, and come to another epochal man—the pioneer of the next endeavor—one also created by the emergency, and who feared not to meet its issues: to take Wycliffe's place almost in perfect reproduction; but whose work, while it was to bring suffering upon himself to an extent that Wycliffe never knew—even unto exile and martyrdom—was nevertheless destined to remain so vitally wrought into the type and texture and substance of our English Bible as never to pass away in any future revision without an absolute change in the style and character of that Household Word.

This man of the new era was the brave, the rugged, the devoted, the invincible WILLIAM TYNDALE:—" the patriarch," says Plumptre, " in no remote ancestry, of the Authorized Version :" "more than Cranmer and Ridley the hero of the English Reformation." For *himself* he appeared as a reformer a few years too soon, but for his *work*, just in time. It was in the beginning of the reign of Henry the Eighth that he became known, and before there was the least tendency on the part of that monarch to break with the Papal power. The king, who was a second son, and had been educated by his father in theology, that he might become Archbishop of Canterbury, prided himself upon his knowledge of divinity. He had even written a book in defence of the Papal authority, for which the Pope had given him the title of "Defender of the Faith." But on the other hand he looked kindly on the "New Learning," and did not share the prejudice of the schoolmen against it. Cardinal Wolsey, also, was a munificent patron of letters, and Tunstal, Bishop of London, was a fine scholar in Latin, Greek and Hebrew. Still there was no sign of the Reformation movement in this quarter. The kingdom was pledged to Rome. Even Sir Thomas More remained a rigid and prejudiced Romanist, although in sympathy with the "New Learning."

Luther's version of the Bible. On the continent the situation was widely different. The Reformation had begun, and had grown into stupendous proportions. Numerous students in Germany had already translated separate books of the Bible, when Luther, single-handed, undertook and accomplished that great Version of the whole Bible which did the same service for his native tongue in fixing its idiom and character, that our version afterwards did for ours. His New Testament appeared in 1522. The whole Bible in 1534, and a revised edition in 1541.

To find Tyndale we must go back to the year 1477, when he was born, in an obscure village of Gloucestershire. He was brought up from a child at Oxford, and became a priest and a Franciscan friar. In his earliest manhood he was "singularly addicted to the study of the Scriptures," and at the age of twenty-five he had translated portions of the New Testament.* While Erasmus resided in Cambridge, 1509–1514, as Professor of Greek, he went himself thither, doubtless drawn by the fame of the great continental scholar. A few years after he returned to Gloucestershire, and became a tutor in the family of a Sir John Welch, at Little Soderby, not far from Bristol. No other spot in England was a greater hot-bed of the Church in its most pretentious and most bigoted form than Gloucestershire at that

<small>Birth and education of Tyndale.</small>

---

* Plumptre. Smith's Bib. Dict. iii. 1668.

time. It was "full of abbots, deans, archdeacons, and divers other doctors and great beneficed men."* Thus was Tyndale surrounded by the Church in its most sumptuous exhibitions of lordly pride. But, like Wycliffe nearly a century and a half before, his familiarity with the Scriptures had so enlarged his views of Divine truth that he was brought into the fiercest antagonism with these arrogant representatives of a corrupt church. His position as a tutor in a wealthy household, much resorted to by them, threw him frequently into their society. He was never prudent of speech in these controversies, chiefly talks at the table, never circumspect and never afraid, and at last he aroused their suspicion and hatred. A single incident, related by Anderson, is characteristic of his whole manner. "Tyndale happening to be in the company of a reputed learned divine, and in conversation having brought him to a point from which there was no escape, he

His controversies with church dignitaries.

---

* Eng. Hexapla 13.

broke up with this exclamation: 'We were better to be without God's law, than the Pope's!' This was an ebullition in perfect harmony with the state of the country at the moment, but it was more than the piety of Tyndale could bear. 'I defy the Pope,' said he, in reply; 'and all his laws; <small>His resolve to translate the Scriptures.</small> and if God spare my life, ere many years, I will cause a boy that driveth the plough to know more of the Scripture than thou dost.'"* This utterance, and his, so-called, heretical attitude generally, brought matters to a crisis. He was no longer safe in Gloucestershire.

But the boast had evidently been <small>The general preparation for the undertaking</small> the outbreak of a secret and long-cherished determination to give the Scriptures to the "lay people." Everything, apparently, was now ready for him. He himself was a ripe scholar in Greek, and a master of English also. The Greek text of the New Testament

---

* Anderson. Annals i. 36. Westcott. Eng. Bib. note 32.

had been published by Erasmus six years before. Luther's translation of it into German was just finished and passing through the press. Abroad a great reformation was shaking the Church. At home, the people were eager to read and to think for themselves, and a wide sympathy with the Continental movement was smouldering among them. All that the poor scholar needed was to be pecuniarily supported while engaged in the work.

He applies to the Bishop of London without success.

So in 1522 he journeyed to London, and, unsophisticated provincial as he was, evidently expected to find the Church differently represented in its dignitaries there. The fame of Tunstal, Bishop of London, as a Greek scholar, and an enlightened patron of the "New Learning," had been trumpeted by Erasmus, and Tyndale therefore sought the Episcopal palace, and opened before the Bishop the plan of the proposed translation. To prove his competency for the task, Tyndale submitted to Tunstal's examination a translation of an oration of Isocrates. But the poor priest, so far from being admitted a member of the episcopal household, was coldly dismissed, and told to look for what he wanted elsewhere in London. He soon found that the spirit of Gloucestershire was in the metropolis also. "I understood at last," writes he, "not only that there was no room in my lord of London's palace to translate the New Testament, but also that there was *no place to do it in all England.*"*

While so dependent and knowing not which way to look or to turn, Monmouth, an alderman of London, a large-hearted and liberal-minded merchant who had heard him preach once or twice, became so practically his friend as to help him with the money necessary for his journey to the Continent— <small>Retires to the Continent.</small> whither accordingly he went, thereafter to live and labor, as he touchingly says, in "poverty, exile, bitter absence from friends, hunger, thirst and cold, great dangers, and in-

---

* Anderson. Annals i. 39.

numerable other hard and sharp fightings."*
His first place of refuge was Hamburg, where, before the end of the year 1524, he translated and published the Gospels of St. Matthew and St. Mark in separate volumes with notes.† Thus amid the ocean of a foreign language the English version began to rise like a coral island, showing itself first above the surface in this rim and ring of an experimental development of a mighty plan.

Issues Matthew and Mark.

From Hamburg he went to Cologne, with his assistant,‡ and set to work upon the entire New Testament, but was interrupted by a spy § upon his movements, and only succeeded in

---

* Westcott. Hist. Bib. 36.

† A forthcoming life of Tyndale, by the Rev. R. Dundas, notices that "no printer is known to have been in Hamburg about these years," in which case the place of the first issue is unknown.—First Printed Eng. New T.—Fac Sim. Pref. 5.

‡ William Roy, author of the satire against Wolsey, "Rede me and be not wrothe."

§ Cochlæus—an exile at Cologne—"a virulent enemy of the Reformation."

saving his papers and printed sheets by a flight by ship up the Rhine, to Worms. <small>Forced to flee to Worms.</small> Here he found a safe refuge in a city, whither only four years before Luther had declared we would go "if there were as many devils in it as there were tiles on the houses." It had now became "wholly Lutheran."

Meantime word was sent to King Henry, Cardinal Wolsey, and Bishop Fisher, of the peril in which England stood. <small>Frightful reports of his work reach England.</small> Dreadful rumors prevailed of a certain Englishman who, at the instance of Luther, had translated the New Testament into English, and who, within a few days, intended "to return with the same imprinted into England," and it would "fill the realm with Lutherans."*

A curious bit of table-talk comes down to us in the diary of a German scholar† dated in this year 1526, which gives us the gossip of the time. After mentioning the discussion of many political and other matters usual at a dinner

---

* Westcott. Hist. Eng. Bible 41.
† Herman von Busche, 11 Aug. 1526.

table of cultivated people, Erasmus and his literary conflicts being one of the topics, he speaks of a person at the table who told him that six thousand copies of the English New Testament had been printed at Worms: that it was translated by an Englishman who lived there with two of his countrymen, who was so complete a master of seven languages, Hebrew, Greek, Latin, Italian, Spanish, English, French, that you would fancy that whichever he spoke in was his mother tongue. He added that the English, in spite of the active opposition of the king, were so eager for the Gospel, as to affirm that they would buy a New Testament even if they had to give a hundred thousand pieces of money for it."*

<small>His stratagem for getting the Version into England.</small> Accompanying the message which had been sent to England, warning the authorities "to prevent the importation of the pernicious article of merchandise," was a description of the quarto

---

* Westcott. Eng. Bible 42. Fac Sim. Text of Tyndale's N. T. 25.

volume which Tyndale was preparing. Not to be foiled in that way, he resorted to an ingenious stratagem for his proposed invasion. He set to work upon another edition, a small octavo, and when it was printed, he returned to the other and completed that also. His plan was that the large volume should attract the attention of the English authorities, and, under cover of that diversion, the unknown small one should slip in among the people. And so it turned out. Both Testaments were shipped to England in number about six thousand, and got into the country. Just at the moment circumstances happened to be propitious. Wolsey was engrossed in state affairs, then in a very critical condition at home and abroad. Tunstal had been sent to Spain on a political mission. The king was keeping Christmas in private. The books were eagerly purchased and became widely but secretly circulated, not only in London, but in Oxford and Cambridge.* It was savagely

<small>Its opposite reception by the people, and by the authorities.</small>

* "The printed English Testaments being ready, there

attacked by high dignitaries both of the church and state. Wolsey advised the king to condemn it to be burnt, which he did. Sir Thomas More, who was especially shocked by the independence of a translation which could ignore all ecclesiastical and technical words, denounced the translation as "ignorant, dishonest, and heretical." * When Tunstal returned he found both editions circulating everywhere in his diocese. He mounted the pulpit of "Paul's Cross," and preached against it, and afterward, in conjunction with the Archbishop of Canterbury, issued a mandate requiring "the collection and surrender of copies."

was a people prepared to receive them. For upwards of a century, amid all manner of national vicissitudes, the Lollards had been multiplying written copies of the original translation of Wycliffe, and of its revised version by John Purvey. They had increased, despite continuous persecution; and were now a scattered unorganized association of tradesmen, craftsmen, and such like, especially numerous in those districts nearest the continent, and therefore most accessible to influences from without." "First Printed Text," 40.

* Westcott. Eng. Bible 42.

All this failing, and more editions coming in, the curious resort was had of buying up the books both in England and on the Continent. But this, of course, was of no avail. The popular interest in the work partook of the nature of a conflagration. It was too widespread to be stamped out. It was too fierce and earnest wherever it burned, to be quenched. The act of purchasing the editions was only pouring oil on that seat of the fire, the printing press of Tyndale. The whole power of the British throne could not extirpate the book. A secret organization was formed to receive and shelter it.* Every device was employed in importing it, so that by the year 1530 six

---

* "These Testament Circulators deserve to be held in perpetual honor. They were Anti-Papists before the Testaments arrived in the country. They instinctively saw in them the great instruments of deliverance of the people from priestly thraldom that weighed so heavily upon them; and at the hazard of their worldly health and wealth they devoted themselves to the dangerous work of their distribution far and wide."—First Printed Text—Fac Simile 47.

editions of fifteen thousand copies were spread throughout England. And yet if there had been no further multiplication of them, even this great number had not been enough to withstand the endeavors to destroy them, for, so persistent and thorough was the search, that to-day only a mutilated fragment or two remains of all this multitude of copies.*

---

* Anderson. Westcott. Hist. Eng. Bib. 45.

"The most valuable of the late old English reprints is unquestionably the choice photolithograph perfect fac simile of the *Unique Fragment of the first printed English New Testament, translated by* William Tyndale. It was probably executed at Cologne in 1525. Its existence was long doubted until the discovery of the precious fragment containing Tyndale's "Prologge" and the Gospel of St. Matthew only, by Mr. Thomas Rodd, the bookseller. It was purchased by Mr. Grenville, and now forms the most precious article of the library bequeathed to the British Museum. It is difficult to estimate the value of a nonexistent thing, but it may be safely said that a fine perfect copy would not wait long for a purchaser at 10,000*l*. in England, and very likely America might dispute its possession. The reprint, most completely edited by Mr. Edward Arber, contains a full examination of the very

But the sturdy translator across the Channel kept his printers at work, and the steady stream of imported Testaments ceased not. They came even on in the grain-ships, for England was then starving as much for food as for the bread of life.

During all this, when he found that the opposition was in great part personal, owing to certain tracts he had written, and especially to the notes with which his work was accompanied, he offered to withhold the latter, and to let the Scriptures go bare of comment or explanation to the people, promising "never to write more." So free as this was his whole effort of self-interest or of the ambition to propagate his own views. But the translation itself was still

<small>In order to disarm opposition, he omits his "notes and comments."</small>

perplexing literary history of the early versions of William Tyndale and his coadjutor, William Roy, whose labors were so effectually effaced by the Romanist authorities that their story has to be disentangled from the merest fragment of evidence. It forms a small quarto volume, elegantly printed."—"Book-Buyer."

too individual and independent—too clear a mirror for the scarlet woman to admire herself in. It needed the dimness imparted by superstition, tradition, and dogma, before it would suit *her* complexion.

This history would be extended too long if all were told which happened to Tyndale and his work during these thirteen years: the persecutions and annoyances and treacheries which he suffered; well as their detail would illustrate his heroic character and Christian patience. "He had been so harassed with enemies that, as he himself expressed it, 'very death would have been pleasanter to him than life.'"* He was constantly compelled to keep his whereabouts a secret, as his person was never out of danger.

<small>His repeated revisions of his Version.</small> All this time, while working off edition after edition of his New Testament, he was by continual and laborious revision making it more and more perfect. Besides the suggestions of his own mind, he

* Anderson. Annals i. 290.

was always ready to receive and adopt hints for its improvement from whatever source they might come, taking an inspiration here and there from Luther's version, and a correction now and then from the Vulgate or the Latin version of Erasmus.

But his labors were not confined to the New Testament. He had, at quite an early part of this period, set to work also upon the more voluminous Hebrew Old Testament. Probably he had acquired a knowledge of Hebrew before he left England, but doubtless he had perfected his acquaintance with it in his wanderings through Hamburg, Cologne, Worms, and Antwerp, cities then filled with Jews, and men famous for Hebrew learning *He undertakes a Version of the Old Testament.*

In 1530* he issued a translation of Genesis and Deuteronomy, just as he had before two

---

* The year before he was shipwrecked on the coast of Holland while on the way to get part of the Old Testament printed, losing his MS. and money. Encyc. Britannica xiv. 400.

Issues Genesis and Deuteronomy, and finally the whole Pentateuch and Jonah.

of the Gospels, in separate volumes. Soon after he published the entire Peutateuch. Three years later appeared the Book of Jonah. He never got further with this part of his undertaking (except some manuscript translations), and it was left to other hands to finish. That which interrupted him was a call to martyrdom.

A great change in England— Henry breaks with the Pope.

But, some time before this took place, a great change had come in England. The king had dissolved his relations with the Pope, and the Church of England had resumed her ancient independence. A kinder feeling grew on the part of Henry and his counsellors toward the project of an English version; for its production would strengthen the king's position with the people and help to alienate his realms from Rome. It is a significant incident which we hear, of

Anne Boleyn's interposition.

the Protestant Queen, Anne Boleyn, saving from punishment a man who had been especially active in circulating the New Testament. And after awhile, when the news of her auspicious influence reached Tyndale, we find him preparing a magnificent copy of his New Testament, sumptuously printed and illuminated on vellum, and splendidly bound, and sending it to her with her royal name inscribed in crimson letters on its gilded edges. This book is still to be seen in the British Museum, and Mr. Plumptre speaks of passages in it underscored in red ink, "such as might be marked for devotional purposes." *

Before he died Tyndale had the satisfaction of hearing that the royal English printer, belonging to the party of the queen, was preparing to issue an edition in London of his own last revised Testament. It appeared after his death. In this way only did the exile return to his native land, but it was a return more sweet to him in the crowning of his life's work than any personal freedom to which he might have attained. *That* he never had again. The man who, as Anderson

An edition preparing by the royal printer.

---

* Smith. Dict. Bib. iii. 1669.

says, "had been deemed of such importance that he had enjoyed the distinction of having been pursued by the agent of Wolsey the cardi-

<small>Tyndale betrayed and imprisoned.</small>

nal, and of the king himself, of Sir Thomas More the Lord Chancellor, and even Cromwell, the future vicegerent,"* was at last overtaken by treachery—a treachery singularly Judas-like in being a betrayal by a trusted friend—arrested, and imprisoned in the castle of Vilvorde near Brussels.

<small>Cranmer's attempt to issue a new Version.</small>

While he lay there, in his living tomb, his spirit was having even another strange apparition at home. The time was already growing so rapidly ripe for an English version that Cranmer, now Archbishop of Canterbury, had carried a resolution through Convocation that the Bible should be translated, and he took what is supposed to be by some Tyndale's New Testament, by others Wycliffe's, and cutting it into eight or ten parts, sent the fragments to as many "best-learned bishops," requesting that they should be

* Anderson. Annals i. 417.

returned corrected on a certain day at Lambeth Palace. But the result was unsatisfactory, and Cranmer gave up the attempt in that quarter. The fact, however, of such an attempt is an indication of the great change of sentiment among the English authorities.

The famous Thomas Cromwell, King Henry's wise and able pilot in all these troublous times, when the English Church was tacking off the lee-shore of Rome, now saw his opportunity and turned the helm in that direction. But the account of this belongs to the next stage of this history. It is enough to say that before Tyndale died he beheld the unfinished portions of the Old Testament completed by another and friendly hand, that of Miles Coverdale, his own translation retouched by the same skilful fingers (though sometimes blended too much with other phraseology), and the *whole Bible,* including so much of his own massive and splendid contribution, enter England, with no voice, royal or ecclesiastical, raised

<small>Cromwell's attempt.</small>

<small>Coverdale's Version.</small>

against it, his name, to be sure, sunk out of sight for the sake of appearances, but his immortal work standing unshaken, to become, for ever after, the adopted form of the future English Bible, the type of its architecture and the material of its construction.

<small>Tyndale executed.</small> But while the gift was received, the giver was more than unacknowledged. He was persecuted now to his death. Through English counsel, solicitation, and management, the Emperor Charles the Fifth issued a decree under which Tyndale was led forth from his dungeon, conducted to a neighboring eminence, tied to a stake, but mercifully strangled before he was burnt to ashes. The last words that escaped from him before the agony of suffocation was a prayer for his countrymen in a prayer for his king: "Lord, open the King of England's eyes!"

<small>The character of Tyndale.</small> The character of Tyndale may be safely said to be one of the noblest in Christian annals. It is the best part of his record that no faction or sect ever

gathered under his name. Self-exiled from his country, he was also an exile from himself. Positive and aggressive as he was in his many writings and pamphlet conflicts, and the notes which at first accompanied his translation, yet he was singularly impersonal and self-forgetful in it all. If he had had more of worldly wisdom and less unsophisticated trust in men, the base betrayal which finally destroyed him would not have been possible. He was a man altogether given up to the thought which moved him, and there is enough in his writings and in his life to prove that if the great object to which he had devoted all, had been attained, namely, the opening of the Scriptures to the glad entrance of the poorest and humblest of his countrymen, he would have been willing to have died, as he did die, in the simple happiness of that unshared consciousness. No public plaudits, no royal recognition would have pleased him as well. And so, with all his publicity, he kept himself really inconspicuous. He was like one who had been the projector of a great edifice, but who was content to secretly inspire its style of architecture and let it appear to be the suggestion of other and more accepted minds. His consciousness of success was his best reward.* And even thus he now appears: one of the

---

* "Tyndale saw his life's work accomplished. Ere he was taken away, the English ploughboy came to know the Scriptures. * * * Ceaselessly for twelve years, at the least, he labored at his great work; yet, so to speak, in secret: which is one reason for his not having been adequately appreciated by posterity. * * * Much more will some day be known of him. Among the archives of Belgium may yet be found the papers seized in his house at Antwerp by the emperor's attorney when he was captured. * * * And among some English dust-covered collection may still be found such of his manuscripts as, passing into the hands of his Timothy—John Rogers—came over into England. Enough is already ascertained to stimulate in us an unceasing search for any trace of him and an increasing study of his works; and what we already know of his nature and character, of his work and purpose, fully justifies our for ever revering him as the great apostle of our early Reformation." "First Printed Eng. N. T. Fac Simile—Introd. 69, 70.

unnoticed inspirations of a great movement, and, by it, one of the fathers of the Reformation. In looking back we see him standing all alone in his hard and dark and eventful life. Wycliffe had his Lollards, Luther his Lutherans, Calvin his Calvinists, but Tyndale is the father and the name of no sect. He is the father of the English Bible, and his name will remain when all sects and systems shall have passed away.

The first remarkable element of his version was its limpid outflow from the original. *Excellencies and peculiarities of his Version.* It rendered what it found there with no intermixture of personal ideas or church prejudices. At least this was its pure intent. And in this was the very peculiarity which precipitated the wrath of Church and state upon him. He rendered "congregation," not "church;" "elder," not "priest;" "acknowledge," not "confess;" "repentance," not "penance;" "favor," not "grace;" "love," not "charity." These latter technical words, so deeply imbedded in the Roman concrete, were not found in his New Testament, but, on the contrary, the former words, so fresh on the lips, so near the heart of everyday human life. "These simple and faithful renderings," says Anderson, "once read in their connection, shook to its very foundations that fabric which the Chancellor (More) had strained all his powers to defend;"* for it was with Sir Thomas More, the champion of Romanism, that Tyndale had his chief combat in the war of controversy and of pamphlets. As a purely individual production, impressed with the strong features of a nature which had grown up intellectually and spiritually almost alone, and yet which possessed the elements of a singular earnestness, simplicity, and purity, as marking the breaking away of a distinctly independent mind, and its assertion of the truth in perfect insulation from the unscriptural Church, the Version of Tyndale takes its immovable place in the history of the Reformation, and as the controlling influence in

Its individuality and originality.

* Annals i. 281.

all future Versions. "From first to last," says Westcott, "his style and his interpretation are his own, and in the originality of Tyndale is included in a large measure the originality of our English version."* " Notwithstanding," says Anderson, "all the confessed improvements made in our translation of the Bible, large portions in almost every chapter remain verbally the same as he first gave them to his country."† "He established," says Westcott again, "a standard of Biblical translation which others followed. * * * It is even of less moment that by far the greater part of his translation remains intact in our present Bibles, than that his spirit animates the whole. He toiled faithfully himself, and where he failed, he left to those who should come after the secret of success. The achievement was not for one but for many; but he fixed the type according to which the later laborers worked. His influ-

<small>Its influence on the present Version.</small>

---

* Eng. Bib. 210.
† Annals i. 245.

ence decided that our Bible should be popular and not literary, speaking in a simple dialect, and that so by its simplicity it should be endowed with permanence. He felt by a happy instinct the potential affinity between Hebrew and English idioms, and enriched our language and thought for ever with the characteristics of the Semitic mind."*

"To Tyndale," says Plumptre, "belongs the honor of having given the first example of a translation based on true principles, and the excellence of later versions has been almost in exact proportion as they followed his. Believing that every part of Scripture had one sense and one only, the sense in the mind of the writer, he made it his work, using all philological helps that were accessible, to attain that sense. Believing that the duty of a translator was to place his readers as nearly on a level as possible with those for whom the books were originally written, he looked on all the later theological associations that had gathered

* Eng. Bib. 211.

round the words of the New Testament as hindrances rather than helps, and sought, as far as possible, to get rid of them." "In this as in other things, Tyndale was in advance, not only of his own age, but of the age that followed him." "All the exquisite grace and simplicity which have endeared the Authorized Version to men of most opposite tempers and contrasted opinions, is due mainly to his clear-sighted truthfulness."*

The historian Froude gives equally forcible testimony to his version. "The peculiar genius," he says, "if such a word may be permitted, which breathes through it; the mingled tenderness and majesty; the Saxon simplicity, the preternatural grandeur, unequalled, unapproached, in the attempted improvements of modern scholars—all are here, and bear the impress of one man, and that man William Tyndale."†

And finally, listen to Bishop Ellicott, who

---

* Smith's Bib. Dict. iii. 1669.
† Hist. Eng. iii. 84.

to-day is the leading spirit in the new work of revision. Speaking of Tyndale's determination to make it in the simple and homely language of the people, he says: "It is to this steady aim and purpose that the special and striking idiomatic excellence of the Authorized Version is pre-eminently due. To this deep resolve we owe it that our own English version is now what we feel it to be,—a Version speaking to heart and soul, and appealing to our deepest religious sensibilities with that mingled simplicity, tenderness, and grandeur, that make us often half doubt, as we listen, whether Apostles and Evangelists are not still exercising their Pentecostal gift, and themselves speaking to us in the very tongue wherein we were born. Verily we may bless and praise God that Tyndale was moved to form this design, and that he was permitted faithfully to adhere to it, for, beyond doubt, it is to that popular element in his Version not only that we owe nearly all that is best in our present English Testament, but that there remains to this very hour, in the heart of all earnest English people, an absolute intolerance of any changes in the words or phraseology that would tend to obscure this special, and, we may justly say, this providential characteristic. Tyndale not only furnished the type of all succeeding versions, but bequeathed principles which will exercise a preservative influence over the Version of the English Bible, through every change or revision that may await it, until Scriptural revision shall be no longer needed and change shall be no more."*

Aside from the natural aptitude which Tyndale had for his work, there was one circumstance which constituted for him an extraordinary opportunity. It enabled him to be, in his peculiar field, what we find the great poets to have been in theirs. The province opened by him was a fresh discovery, and he had the genius to exhaust very nearly all its treasures. His successors were only gleaners. This favorable *The favorable condition of the English language when it was executed.*

* Revision of Eng. New Testament 60.

circumstance was the condition of the English language at the time in which he lived. It was then going through that long process of its formation, which we saw beginning in Wycliffe's day, in an emergence from the Anglo-Saxon, and transition, through the Latin and Norman-French, and which ended in its becoming a fixed national tongue. It was in its most plastic state, ready for any rich form into which both association and genius might mould it. In addition to this, both of the original languages of the Bible were found to be in most "potential affinity" with it. Tyndale himself discovered this, and states the fact in opposition to the common preference at that time for the Vulgate translation of both Testaments. "The Greek tongue," he says, "agreeth more with the English than the Latin."[*] "And the properties of the Hebrew tongue agree a thousand times more with the English than the Latin. The manner of speaking is in both one, so that in a thousand places

---

[*] Westcott. Eng. Bib. 174.

thou needest not but to translate it into English word for word."* The forming language yielded to the strong peculiarities of the others. Like a plastic substance, it took, under the skilful hands of Tyndale, the stamp and impress of both these dies, the Hebrew, and the Hellenistic Greek. It yielded to the idiom of either, again and again at will, till the style assumed often a foreign and oriental character; and when the people began to read and quote their Bible, its peculiar turns of expression wrought themselves insensibly into the forms of their daily speech, and thus the plain, insular language of England, already composite, and disposed to be more so, became gradually enriched with the native force and beauty of the original tongues of the Scriptures. We ourselves are now daily employing unconsciously the idiom of both the earlier and the later Hebrews, and all because our language at this period of Tyndale melted so easily into both of the ancient and

* Plumptre. Smith's Bib. Dict. iii. 1669.

bygone languages of the Bible. When a man of genius and spiritual intuition had such an untried opportunity as this, what wonder is it that the product of his labor became of everlasting permanence; and what wonder, too, that he succeeded in occupying the field so entirely as to anticipate the future, and leave the work of improving upon him the only office of his successors?

<small>A version should be a direct, impersonal transfer from the original.</small>

We owe still one other matter of inestimable value to the example of Tyndale: namely, the principle that a version of the Bible should be perfectly *colorless*, tinctured with no thought which may previously have had possession of the translator. Even if it should come into being amid the rich embosoming of the church, and within the very walls of her doctrines, still it must take no ecclesiastical, traditional, or conventional form whatever. That which it is in the original it must be in the translation; and this, as we have seen, was the marked element which distinguished the Version of Tyndale, so far as he was able to control it—the element which, at the time, raised against his work the opposition of the church, but which hereafter it will be the very life and protection of the church to reproduce. Our Bible, through the influence of its subsequent revisions, cannot be said to be entirely free of doctrinal prepossessions. It took somewhat the color of the times through which it passed, but the stern, earnest finger of Tyndale still points onward to a day when the effulgence of the originals shall shine upon mankind, not through many-colored lights as of cathedral windows, to keep us all in a "*dim* religious light," but as the sun when it shineth on the face of nature—in their purity and in their strength.

NOTE.—Mr. Blunt, in his "Plain Account of the English Bible," written and published since the late movement towards revision, takes altogether different ground from the scholars quoted in this chapter, and, evidently moved by doctrinal prejudice, like the contemporary ecclesiastics of Tyndale, gives him no place and no credit in the formation of the English Bible. It is a melancholy instance of how a mind can bring itself to ignore palpable facts, in order to make room for its own prepossessions. By him our Version is based on Wycliffe's, and Wycliffe's on previous Versions (though renderings from the Latin), because these Versions took the simple Saxon forms of speech, which characterize our present Bible. Tyndale is abused, slandered, and disowned. Mr. Blunt was born in the reign of Henry the Eighth! What is he doing on earth at the present time? As to the quality of his judgment, it may be mentioned that in a late statement of reasons against revision, the final, and of course the strongest in his mind, is the fact that the English reading public have a "vested right" in the "Authorized Version" as so much *property;* the copies in circulation would be rendered valueless by the issue of another, and thus injustice would be done to the owners! The interests of truth, the full revelation of the Word of God, to be sacrificed to such a consideration as this!

III.

THE SIX LINEAL DESCENDANTS OF TYNDALE'S PATRIARCH-VERSION.

The Bibles of Coverdale, Rogers, Cromwell, Cranmer, Geneva, and the Bishops.—The Greek Testaments of Stephens and Beza.—The Hebrew Text.

THE BIBLE OF COVERDALE.

AS we have seen, Erasmus laid the foundation of the English New Testament in gathering his Greek manuscripts together, and publishing the first Greek Text, and Tyndale reared the superstructure, and fixed for ever its style and architecture. But the latter left, as we have also seen, the scaffolding still standing, and the building, which he had erected in such magnificent masonry, unfinished and rough-hewn,

The work of Erasmus and Tyndale incomplete.

awaiting the finer hands of the carver and gilder before all its glory could be revealed. And like the builders of a great cathedral, whose work still lies down in the crypt and among its supporting archways, which make the security, and in the solid walls of the building above, which mark the character of the fabric, both Erasmus and Tyndale have been almost forgotten in the more effective labors and later ingenuity of their successors.

Many years after the illustrious scholar had passed away, and his equally illustrious colaborer, Cardinal Ximenes, other workmen were found strengthening the foundations and clearing the passages down amid the darkness of a long-dead language. Erasmus and Tyndale closed their labors and their lives almost together. They both died in 1536. About ten years after, in 1546, another workman was prepared to exhibit the result of his labors in the Greek text.

The Greek Text of Stephens. The famous Robert Stephens, a printer of Paris, and a scholar as well, issued a new edition, correcting the work of Erasmus by manuscripts taken chiefly from the French Royal Library.* But the doctors of the Sorbonne persecuted him, and, after issuing two more editions, he went to Geneva and issued another, which is especially notable for a peculiarity with which every one is familiar. It was the first New Testament divided up into verses. This was Stephens's own work, and had been done by him while riding on his mule from Paris to Lyons, in order, it is said, to facilitate the references of a Concordance he was preparing. These divisions, however, were indicated by figures on the margin. He did not venture to break up the paragraphs into the apothegmic little morsels which disfigure our Bibles to-day. This was done in one of the Versions which afterward appeared.

Ten or fifteen years after Stephens had closed his labors Theodore Beza appeared down in the crypt, and *The Greek text of Beza.*

---

* Tregelles. History of the Greek Text of the New Testament, 31.

worked there thirty-three years—1565–98—issuing five editions of his text, correcting the work of Stephens by the aid of still more ancient and valuable manuscripts. And he also, like Erasmus, accompanied it by a Latin translation of his own, intended to exhibit the inaccuracy of the Vulgate. His Text and his version both became favorites with the Protestants. But the Romanists, still unlearned in the field of Greek textual criticism, and as prejudiced as ever, roundly abused this good workman also.

<small>The successors of Tyndale.</small> While these scholars, successors of Erasmus, were thus busy below upon the foundations, and completing the vaulted archways which should securely sustain the pavement above, the successors of Tyndale also were at work upon the superstructure which he had left unfinished. They availed themselves of his plan and his material, and here and there improved, and here and there, but only in slight instances, comparatively, deformed his building. But it was they who, after many

changes, were at last to take down the scaffolding that had stood about it through three generations, and reveal to the world the almost "perfect beauty" which belongs to our present Bible.

In the reader's view of this edifice, during this opening era of its erection, he must not forget to notice the adjoining fabric of the Old Testament, rising also from its still older foundation, the published Hebrew Text, but as yet built not more than a single story above the ground: the five chambers of the Pentateuch complete, and the Book of Jonah standing like a lone column, the last printed work of Tyndale's hands. *Tyndale's work on the Old Testament.*

We return now to the moment when these after-builders entered upon his labors, and began anew upon the structure which he had erected. In 1534 Convocation, with archbishop Cranmer at its head, petitioned king Henry to "graciously indulge unto his subjects of the laity the reading of the Bible in the English tongue—that *Cranmer's first attempt to issue the English Bible.*

a new translation might be forthwith made for that end and purpose." At this time twenty editions of Tyndale's New Testament were in England, circulating secretly under a ban, and others, more recently published, were pouring in. It will be noticed how this petition recognised its existence in this prayer for a "new translation." We have seen the fate of Cranmer's attempt, after permission had been obtained, to get the proposed Version from the bishops. They could not agree upon a Version clear of church trammels and technical words. Their fingers were tied, as their minds were tinged, by theological prepossessions. Each one wore the Latin Vulgate as a pair of spectacles wherewith to read the Greek. And so Cranmer, after receiving their prejudiced and variant suggestions, gave up the task as something which could not be had from that quarter " till," to use his own words, " the day after doomsday."

<small>Cromwell's first attempt.</small> But Thomas Cromwell, then rapidly rising to the height of his

power and influence, the great manager of the English Reformation in its earlier stages, wisely and quickly seized the opportunity which was yet open, of advancing the progress of English independence of the Papal power.

It was desirable, if the work of translating should fall again into the hands of an individual, in default of any present ability in the church authorities to agree upon an English Version, that it should come from one who, unlike Tyndale, had not made himself obnoxious in any way to them, especially to the king, and who was of a nature compliant enough to accommodate his translation temporarily to the situation. Whether or not the peculiar gifts required, were actually discovered and noticed in one person, and led to his connection with the undertaking, or were afterward developed by himself, certainly the successor of Tyndale was astonishingly well fitted to meet the necessity as it stood. There is a mystery in his movements which may have been accidental, but

Coverdale.

which probably was designed, in the conniving action of Cromwell and others. All we know is that Miles Coverdale, at one time a priest and an Augustine friar, but early in sympathy with the Reformation, and, about the time of Tyndale's first issue, intimately connected with Cromwell and More, was the singularly qualified man by whom the great work was undertaken at this critical moment. By taste, talent and preference a preacher, yet the finger of Providence, either in the suggestion of Cromwell or the monitions of his own heart, probably both, seemed to point to this arduous and unwonted task. Four or five years before this, he had met Tyndale at Hamburg, and some say he had a hand in assisting the pioneer. Doubtless he there imbibed an intense interest in the translation then proceeding. It is very likely when the change came over the Church of England, that he understood the situation, and that Cromwell also understood *him*. At any rate he is found, just at this period, self-exiled on the continent, no one knows where, engaged with tremendous energy on the work of preparing not only another New Testament, but the whole Bible for the English public. The tireless industry with which he must have labored is indicated by the fact that he completed the stupendous work and had it printed in eleven months!

He reproduced all Tyndale's New Testament, and the portions of the Old Testament already executed, revising them with a rich infusion of his own paraphrastic style, (but sometimes rendering very felicitously), and then added the remainder in a very free version. Whether it was part of his accommodating tact, or whether it was the simple fact, he did not pretend to have produced his Version from the originals but, by a kind of distillation, to have gathered and concentrated the riches of five other translations into his own. "I have," he says in his dedication, "purely and faithfully translated this out of five sundry interpreters." Two of these were

Coverdale issues the whole Bible.

Latin Versions, two German, and the other was very probably Tyndale's. His knowledge of Hebrew and Greek enabled him to discriminate in a selection of renderings, and his command of English gave him occasionally most happy turns of expression. Many of these subtle changes remain in our present translation, adding much to its force and beauty. His Version was thus a composite piece of architecture, introduced to complete the edifice of the Bible, and was made to unite and blend itself with the grand but simple structure of Tyndale.

<small>Characteristics of his Version.</small> But the work of Coverdale, when finished and published, developed an individual character of its own. It was too free and paraphrastic for accuracy, but was, nevertheless, smooth, rich, and rhythmical. "Though he is not original," says Westcott,* " yet he was endowed with an instinct of discrimination which is scarcely less precious

---

* Hist. Eng. Bib. 217.

than originality, and a delicacy of ear which is no mean qualification for a popular translator." "Our admiration for the solitary massive strength of the one (Tyndale) must not make us insensible to the patient labors and tender sympathy of the other."*

The Psalter in the Book of Common Prayer as compared with the more literal rendering of the Psalms in the Authorized Version is a very fair specimen of the way in which he executed the entire Bible.

His contribution to our present Version may be summed up, first, in certain peculiar felicities of expression, and next in the general result of a quickness to avail himself of the suggestions of other masters of the original tongues.

But, in another point, the Version, in his hands, took a step backward into the old ecclesiastical preoccupation, and many of the words which Tyndale had so independently

* Hist. Eng. Bib. 70.

rendered, were changed in order to better suit the time.

<small>Utility of a diversity of translations.</small> The distinguishing element of strength and wisdom in Coverdale was his belief in a diversity of translations, in the consultation of many minds, and in the greater wealth that could be given to a Version which combined the impressions received by different scholars from the self-same original passage; variations not in essence, but in light and color. "One translation," he says, "declareth, and openeth, and illustrateth another, and in many places one is a plain commentary unto another." It is this principle which ought to enter into any other Version and revision, and bring about the introduction of a marginal *variorum* of renderings, so that the reader may learn to gather the sense with the mind as well as with the eye, and to catch the living spirit more than to weigh the inadequate letter of any secondary form in which God's word may come to him. This principle is already realized

somewhat, but not by any means enough, in the marginal renderings inserted in our present Bible.

Such is all we owe to Coverdale. His Version had its own great use, and it was only such a one, pretending so little to be an original production, and accommodating itself so skilfully to the temper of the time, that could have hoped to get the king's approval, and attain to an *open* circulation among the people.

When it was published in 1535,— less than ten years after Tyndale's first issue,—with a dedicatory letter to the king, it was allowed by the authorities to go where it would, and, in about two years, another edition appeared with "the king's most gracious license." So at last the Scriptures were no longer secretly published and read in England. Coverdale's Bible licensed by the king.

Thus far we have the whole Bible produced, and with such a curious paternity: by two men so picturesquely opposite and yet complemental to each other, and both so fitted to their opportunity: the strong, Tyndale and Coverdale compared.

the positive, the uncompromising, the original Tyndale: the amiable, the negative, the complying, the skilful Coverdale: the one introducing the true type of what a version should be, and boldly presenting it in advance of his time: the other clothing it with an illusive vesture, which softened its outlines and brought it without suspicion into the precincts of the court and the church. The one was the sun, giving a positive and original light; the other, the moon giving the lustre of the former, but in a diminished radiance: each rising in his turn, to illumine the Scriptures in order that the people might read the Word of God.

Tyndale died at the stake, a martyr to the cause of the Bible. Coverdale lived to see it rise from the ashes of that martyrdom, to witness its eventful progress, to follow, and even to participate in its future history, to behold his own imperfect work superseded, and yet to labor with splendid energy on the better work that was to come.

THE BIBLE OF ROGERS.

Two years after Coverdale's successful and unopposed introduction of the whole Bible, another Version, in large folio, entered England, and received a greeting as strange and cordial as it might be supposed to have been unexpected. The afterward famous martyr, John Rogers, then an eminent divine, and a chaplain to an English mercantile society at Antwerp, a companion of Tyndale, and well known to be his friend and co-laborer, printed abroad and sent over to England a Bible, which was made up of Tyndale's Version of the New Testament, and of the already mentioned portions of the Old, as it was before Coverdale's revision, and also of Coverdale's individual Version of the remainder.* The characteristic contributions of

_{John Rogers. His Version a revision of Tyndale and Coverdale. Its success.}

---

* This Bible was known at the time, as "Matthews's Bible," from the name of Thomas Matthews having been allowed to appear conspicuously in it. The name was either a pseudonym for Rogers or represented the person who bore the cost of the work.

the two were united, but not, as before, blended. Tyndale stood out for himself, and Coverdale for himself. Well as it had answered its temporary purpose, Coverdale's Bible was not yet satisfactory to scholars, however popular it may have been with the people. To the latter it must have been acceptable, for it passed through edition after edition for eighteen years. But a scholar like archbishop Cranmer felt too sensibly its lack of distinctness and close fidelity to the original not to be anxious that another Version should be forthcoming. And so, strangely enough, reappeared this New Testament of Tyndale, with hardly an alteration, with even his formidable initials W. T. curiously flourished in one part, and with even some of his obnoxious notes, and yet by the petition of Cranmer, and by the influence of Cromwell the king's express license was procured for it.

As the Bible of Coverdale would seem to have come in by the management of the statesman Cromwell, so the Bible of Rogers appears to have entered under the encouragement of the prelate Crammer. His delight, when he received the first copy, was unbounded, and he did not rest till he had secured, through Cromwell, the full authorization of the king. "A copy was ordered by royal proclamation to be set up in every church. This was therefore the first Authorized Version." *

At this point, the building, stripped, as to Tyndale's part, of Coverdale's alterations and decorations, and, as to Coverdale's part, left quite as its author had produced it, stands up a singular composite of two styles, no longer intermingled, but side by side,—and, from this moment, begins that more systematic and uninterrupted improvement of each, which, in about seventy-five years, was to result in our present Bible.

margin: Rogers's Bible the starting point of all subsequent rev'sions.

* Plumptre. Smith's Bib. Dict. iii. 1671.

THE BIBLE OF CROMWELL.

<small>Cromwell's second attempt.</small> Cromwell was now vicegerent.* (1536.) There were already four Versions in the field: Tyndale's, Coverdale's, Rogers's, and one by Taverner a noted lay scholar. Many thousands of these were in circulation, but still none were entirely satisfactory. Besides internal deficiencies, they were burdened with polemical notes or commentaries, designed to throw a color over the Version they accompanied. Cromwell projected a new Bible on a magnificent scale. This time it should not creep up to the throne, but should come from the throne. There was no press in England worthy to execute it. In Paris there were more excellent materials and

---

* "Cromwell had been the secretary of Wolsey. His advocacy of his master, in the hour of his fall, is a memorable instance of noble fidelity,—his love of the Scriptures was early proved by his learning the whole of Erasmus's Latin Testament by heart,—and his preference for the reformed religion was unquestionably decided."—*English Hexapla* 21.

more skilful workmen. Francis the First, in his zeal for fine printing, had founded the Royal Printing House, the types of which have been celebrated ever since. Moved by Cromwell, king Henry applied to king Francis for permission to have the forthcoming Bible printed at this Royal Press in the University of Paris, which was granted. Now again appears Coverdale, called upon Coverdale again. a second time by Cromwell to engage in the great undertaking, and this time, under these better auspices, to issue a new Version on the basis of Rogers's, and of course to supersede his own, then quite as popular as any other. It was characteristic of the man to forget himself in the great cause, and he accordingly departed for Paris, taking with him Grafton, a printer of London, who had already made great efforts to secure the exclusive royal right to publish Rogers's Bible, but without success.

Coverdale and Grafton, reviser and printer, had got well on with their work, when Roman Catholic jealousy Romanists in Paris interrupt the work.

overtook them. The inquisitor-general of France ordered the presses to stop, and the sheets to be seized. The Englishmen had to flee, but they had already taken the precaution to remove the larger part of what they had done to England. Not long after they returned and succeeded in conveying presses, type, and even workmen to London, and four great dry vats full of sheets, which had been condemned to be burned, but which had instead been sold as waste paper. Thus, what at first appeared to be a great misfortune turned out to be a great benefit; for, by this importation of material and skill, a new impetus was given to the art of printing in England, and the Bible could thenceforth be altogether a home production.

The Great Bible. Cromwell's Bible was finished and published in 1539. It appeared in a large and mighty folio, and was distinguished by the name of " The Great Bible." A significant cut appeared on the title-page, designed by Holbein, representing the king on his throne, with a group of ecclesiastics on the right hand, and a group of nobles on the left, to each of which the king is handing a volume labelled in Latin "The Word of God." Below the ecclesiastics stands archbishop Cranmer, and below the nobles vicegerent Cromwell, both also engaged in distributing the Holy Bible. This Bible went to the people without note or comment; and so far it was the sole enterprise of Cromwell.

THE BIBLE OF CRANMER.

The next year, 1540, Cranmer himself undertook the work, and *Cranmer's revision of it.* issued under his own name, as archbishop of Canterbury, a revision of Cromwell's Bible, in which there were so many changes that the issue merits a distinct place in the chain of Versions.* It was published, like its predecessor, in stupendous folio, under the same skilled direction, and from the types which had been brought from Paris. In other superficial respects, also, it resembled its predecessor, and was

---

* English Hexapla, 29.

also known as "The Great Bible." One marked feature, however, distinguished it: an elaborate Preface, foreshadowing the true ideal of a version, written by the archbishop. There is now in the British Museum "a splendid copy of it, on vellum, with the cuts and blooming letters curiously illuminated." This was the gift of Cranmer to his royal master.

Its use enjoined by the king. The popular delight. Simultaneously with the appearance of the Great Bible a royal decree enjoining its use was issued, which was ordered "to be set up upon every church door," and given to the clergy to read to their congregations. There was not a little feeling against this act of the king among many of these ecclesiastics, and not a few endeavors to make it of none effect, but with no success. The people were not slow in seizing their advantage and manifesting their delight. Six copies of the Great Bible had been set up in St. Paul's, chained to as many desks, for public reading. Crowds gathered round each, listening eagerly to the loud tones of some one able to read in a sufficiently clear voice to be heard by all. An old author gives us a graphic picture of the public enthusiasm at this time. "It was wonderful to see," he says, "with what joy this book of God was received not only among the learneder sort and those that were noted for lovers of the Reformation, but generally all England over among all the vulgar and common people; and with what greediness God's Word was read, and what resort to places where the reading of it was. Everybody that could bought the book, or busily read it, or got others to read it to them if they could not themselves, and divers more elderly people learned to read on purpose. And even little boys flocked among the rest to hear portions of the Holy Scripture read."*

St. Paul's Cathedral, as may be imagined, beheld many a noisy scene about this time. Crowds of people gathered round its six desk-chained Bibles to listen to those among them who were educated enough

Scenes in St. Paul's.

* Strype, in Westcott's Hist. Eng. Bib. 107.

to read the black-letter text, and neither the readers nor the hearers seem to have had much regard for the regular uses of the place in their eagerness to read and to hear the Word of God for themselves. It mattered not at what hour it was,—the hour of prayer, or the hour of high mass,—they flocked round their Bibles, and the loud voices of their lay readers, with their own earnest comments, sometimes drowned the voices of the priests officiating before the altar. So, under the very roof of the cathedral, the revolutionary uproar of the people crowding to the fresh fountains of living water, and the choral tones of a service still conducted in Latin, and therefore appearing like buckets for ever ascending but bringing nothing up, came into discordant conflict, and miniatured the general antagonism of the time. The church and the people were not yet in full sympathy. A wilful, fickle monarch, full of royal humors, not protestant principles, at heart a catholic, only in policy no papist, had granted this inconsistent liberty to his subjects; and the church, also divided as to its own counsels, in one part of it stood in opposition, resistance, and complaint, and in the other part of it tried to accommodate itself to the situation, to meet the people half way in their newly found freedom, and to gather them once more into the fold of the primitive church— the church as it was, before the Romish development began to turn what was intended to be a refuge of safety into a house of bondage.

Cromwell and Cranmer had this latter work in hand. But the time drew near when the one was to be broken before the royal will, and the other had to bend. Cromwell perished at the block; and, when the Bible was to be printed again, his coat-of-arms ignominiously disappeared from the title-page, and the names of Bishops Tunstal and Heath, his opponents, appeared with that of Cranmer, to give credit to the edition.

Thus it happened, in less than twenty years from the day in which the poor scholar Tyndale applied at the palace

Posthumous triumph of Tyndale.

of Tunstal for his patronage in translating the Scriptures, and was coldly dismissed; in less than fifteen years from the days in which "my lord of London" was collecting, purchasing, and burning the Testaments of Tyndale; Tunstal is found putting his name on the title-page of what was still substantially that martyr's work. A later edition still exhibits Cranmer bending, as was his policy, before the formidable humors of the king, and in his Preface taking that neutral tint which enabled the Great Bible "to keep its ground during the changing moods of Henry's later years."

Edward VI. Greater freedom to the Bible in any Version. Parliament, at this moment, proscribed Tyndale's translation; and the king prohibited all other editions and forms of the Bible, Coverdale's included, leaving only the Great Bible unforbidden. And even the reading of this was restricted by decrees to certain classes of the people, during this strange reaction of the royal mind. In the midst of it all, however, Henry died, 1547, and was succeeded by his son, Edward the Sixth. Then

the tide set strongly the other way, and the reforming party were afloat again. It is said that the Great Bible was even used at his coronation. A chronicler writes, "When three swords were brought, signs of his being king of three kingdoms, he said there was one yet wanting. And when the nobles about him asked him what that was, he answered, '*The Bible.*' 'That Book,' added he, 'is the Sword of the Spirit, and to be preferred before these swords.' And when the pious young king had said this, and some other like words, he commanded the Bible with the greatest reverence to be brought and carried before him."*
If the boy-king was crammed by Cranmer, probably this actually took place. At any rate the utmost freedom of publication was decreed, and in this short reign of six years and a half, thirty-five editions of the New Testament, and thirteen editions of the whole Bible were printed. The people were allowed to exercise their preference for Tyndale's, Coverdale's,

* Westcott. Hist. Eng. Bib. 116.

Taverner's, or Cranmer's versions. Instead of restrictions limiting to the educated class the right of reading the Scriptures, "the public use of them was made the subject of admonition and inquiry."* The people were exhorted to read.

<small>Formation of the Prayer-Book.</small> Meanwhile a new labor fell to Cranmer, which, in its turn, engrossed his attention as a matter of the next importance. This was the constitution of the English Church and the remoulding of the Service Books. Now commenced the formation of the Book of Common-Prayer, like the birth of a sister, following the already sturdy youth of her elder brother the English Bible. Even at this stage of their growing together we can find the lineaments of a family likeness between them. The "Psalter" version of the Psalms was taken from the Great Bible of Cranmer, and has been allowed to remain through all the repeated revisions of the Prayer-Book, because of its better adaptation to choral rendering.

* Westcott. Hist. Eng. Bib. 116.

It was declared to be "smoother and more easy to sing." The familiar sentences in the Communion office,* also, continue as they were in the Great Bible, and are to us the footsteps, yet unobliterated, of the Bible as it was then passing on to a period of greater perfection. Those old standards and authorities of church doctrine, the "Homilies," also, are thick-strewn with like vestiges of this period, for all their quotations of Scripture are from this Bible of Cranmer.

But the next historic vicissitude was close at hand, to cut short the labors of the English Reformers on the Prayer Book, and to bring another stifling but brief epoch upon the Bible they had given to the church. Edward died, and was succeeded by his Roman Catholic sister, Mary. Cranmer and Rogers now went to the stake. Coverdale, who had been made Bishop of Exeter, fled to the continent. The Bible was removed from

The persecution under Mary.

---

* Westcott says that these were independently translated by Cranmer from the Latin.

9

the churches, which had become Roman Catholic again. Everything fell back into the old condition of the time of Tyndale. The Bible printing presses were stopped. The Bibles were burnt. The crown, the cardinal, and the bishops were again in array against them, and the people were again obliged to keep their precious treasure concealed.

<small>The revision of the Bible at Geneva.</small> Once more was the undertaking of Scriptural revision driven into exile, to gather new strength for its next invasion of England. Of admitted imperfection, as it stood, even by Cranmer himself, and looking to another revision which should satisfy scholars by diminishing the infusion of Coverdale's too free phraseology, the Great Bible was destined to be superseded by another magnificent contribution, which should bring the Version a long step further on toward the point of perfection so anxiously desired. And this next stage in the interesting progress was not in the line of the English Church, for the English Church lay under suppression:

smouldering in the ashes of the martyrs. The Version that now appeared was made under the lantern of John Calvin. It came from the Puritans and Presbyterians of Geneva, and proved to be one of the *Its remarkable merit.* wisest and greatest of the translations, one of the noblest of the tributaries which joined the swelling river, bringing a wealth in its alluvium of renderings by which the Bible will always be enriched; and yet on account of one unfortunate peculiarity in its editing, creating a *ripple* in the smooth current of its language by which the pellucid meaning of the original beneath is almost hopelessly disturbed. This was the breaking up of the paragraphs into verses. But the account of a translation of such marked origin, influence, and character, of which it can be truly said that it was "for sixty years the most popular of all Versions," a formidable rival for nearly a generation of our present Bible, competing with that consummate work of the church, even after its own best elements had been incorporated therein, an exile from England and produced independently of the church,—the account of such a translation may well open the next stage of this chapter of Bible history and conduct it to its close. We have so far seen the Providential influence of individualism in Tyndale, of eclecticism in Coverdale, of ecclesiasticism in Cranmer; and now we shall see the influence of Puritanism (or independency), in the Version of Geneva, of the Established Church (or authority), in the Version of the Bishops, and finally of the best catholicity that was then attainable in the Version of the King.

THE BIBLE OF GENEVA.

The product of independent minds. As the best beginning for the translation of the Bible proved to be an individual version, for, in that, was reached the fixed character of its structure, so the best contribution to its subsequent improvement came from independency. And, at that time, the conditions of both were persecution and exile. Thirty years after the lone Tyndale's Version appeared—in 1557–60—another of almost equally marked character came forth from the press of Geneva, the city of Calvin and Beza, and was executed chiefly, as to the New Testament, by one man, (William Whittingham, a brother-in-law of Calvin) but not in loneliness, nor in poverty, nor want of sympathy; for a company of scholars, including Coverdale, assisted him. Calvin himself penned the Introduction, and the congregation of exiles, with enthusiastic generosity, paid for the printing, which was beautifully done, and with ideal sentiment, from silver type.*

It was the persecution under Mary which had brought about this expatriation of such a number of English people, and it was the presence of Calvin which produced this concentration of non-conforming Biblical students and others at Geneva. "For the first time," says Westcott,

<small>Providential advantages.</small>

---

* Anderson. Annals of the Eng. Bib. ii. 307.

"the task of emendation was undertaken by men who were ready to press it to the uttermost. They spoke of their position as Providential, and in looking back upon the later results of their Bible, we can thankfully acknowledge that it was so."* "Seeing," they say in their Preface, "the great opportunity and occasions which God presented unto us in this Church, by reason of so many and godly men and such diversity of translations in divers tongues, we undertook this great and wonderful work, which our God according to His divine Providence hath directed to a most prosperous end." Their advantages had been, besides the material already accumulated, certain new Versions in German and Latin, especially the latter of Beza. They had around them also a group of scholars who were engaged in correcting the French Version; which Calvin, by the way, revised three times in thirteen years. The basis of their work was the Great Bible of Cranmer. Origi-

* Hist. Eng. Bib. 272.

nal and independent as it was, it was still, like all its predecessors, only a revision. A readiness to accept suggestions from this and that quarter, and to avail themselves of the assistance of many minds, would seem to have been the humble and true principle of the translators. And this principle of conference and consultation afterward grew into the appointment of companies of scholars, commissioned to execute the work, as we shall see in the case of the two remaining Versions which complete the series.

Certain it is that no other Version except the present one has had more the decided approval of learned men. Probably every one qualified to judge will endorse the declaration of Mr. Scrivener, one of the most careful and accurate authorities of the age, who has minutely investigated its critical value. "It is not too much to say," he writes, "that their (the Geneva translators') Version is the best in the English language, with the single exception of the Authorized Bible."

Characteristics which gave it success. Besides its wonderful merit as revealing more of the force and meaning of the originals than any preceding translation, it had certain other marked features. Hitherto the Bibles which had come out by royal license, and been ordered to be set up in the churches, had been produced on too stately a scale, and with a certain safe leaning backwards, even in mechanical form and execution, which is characteristic of all official authorizations, but which is too slow and hesitating to suit the spirit of activity and progress. The Bibles of Coverdale, Cromwell, and Cranmer had all appeared in ponderous, unwieldy folios, and were printed in black-letter, a type then unpopular and not easily read. The more free and independent issue of the Genevan scholars, who were not hampered by the heavy machinery of church and state, was a product which assimilated itself, externally as well as internally, with the spirit of the age and the mind of the people. It had no royal or ecclesiastical reluctance to declare itself thoroughly; either in the fearless renderings of its text, or in any necessary departure from the traditional proprieties of publication which might bring it the nearer to the popular heart. Its first purpose was *to be read and understood*. And, therefore, more than any other Version, it succeeded in reaching the hearths and homes of England. Instead of appearing in tremendous and expensive folio, it came out in a comparatively small and cheap quarto. Instead of wearing the ancient and obsolescent vesture of black-letter, it went among the people in the every-day garb of the roman character.

In addition to this, its margins were full of condensed and telling comments, which seemed to elicit the spiritual meaning of passages still obscure in the translation. Of course these marginal interpretations were somewhat Calvinistic. A subsequent edition was accompanied by an excellent Bible Dictionary—another most wise provision for its entire intelligibility.

Its Bible Dictionary.

An unfortunate novelty. The paragraphs broken into verses.

Another element of its adaptation to the people, while at the time well calculated to make it effective, afterward proved to be a most unfortunate innovation, and this feature has come down even to us as a heritage, which to-day, instead of making the Bible popular and readable, rather makes it unpopular and unreadable, besides giving it in an unessential respect a peculiarity among other books. This is the breaking up of the paragraphs into the fragments called "verses" or "texts." It was never done until this Genevan version did it. At first, as we have seen, it was only a device of a printer of a Greek Testament to facilitate reference, and the figures were placed on the margin, while the page remained as it was written. Now, however, the Bible appeared, broken into these minute portions, and such an intense and individual look was given to each of them, that they seemed to be pithy expressions, full of their own meaning, apart from any paragraphical connection, like proverbs, aphorisms, and wise sayings. These came to be quoted as separate utterances, and were balanced against or combined with similar apothegms to be found elsewhere in the Holy Book, and, as a consequence, the mental habit set in of catching the meaning of the Bible by a comparison and collection of these detached portions, more than by apprehending the current thought of the writings as they were continuously read. It became an effort to follow the thread of an argument or extended statement with these incessant breaks in the texture. The Bible might have remained clear to a mind which could overlook them, but this innovation furnished too often an occasion for the uncultivated intellect to stumble and to stop, and then to form conceptions and theories, and finally build doctrines out of this broken material which otherwise would never have had such a suggestion. Sectarianism has found any amount of opportunity amid these unfortunate schisms in the simple text of the Scriptures. We cannot thank the Puritan Presbyterian Bible, therefore, for this novelty. But, at the time, it was wisely contrived to enhance the popularity of the new Version; and little did its authors dream of its ultimate abuse.

The Apocrypha omitted. One other peculiarity of the Genevan Version may be mentioned as having had an effect in the present time. It was the first to omit the apocryphal books, and therefore few Bibles now contain them. The Apocrypha, while properly not canonical, has become too rare and is too little read. It yet retains, however, its place in the official Bible of the English Church, not as an authority, but as containing a certain splendor of truth and a practical wisdom, in many portions, which the church "would not willingly let die."

Accession of Elizabeth. Return of the Bible to England in the Genevan Version. The Genevan Version, originating in so many peculiar providences, and developed by so much spiritual insight, found, in the evolution of its good fortune, the time already ripe for its issue and reception. "Bloody Mary" had just died, and the protestant Elizabeth had ascended the throne of England. At the first, indeed, it would seem as if it were threatened with Tyndale's experience over again, for, having been printed a few months before Mary's death, the ports of England were shut against it. But the change to Elizabeth suddenly opened the whole country to the return of the exiles with their noble achievement.

When the Version entered England it came of course with a "Dedication to the Queen," for that was in accordance with the custom of the time. But it came also with another significant innovation: *an Address to the People.*

The coronation ceremonies and pageant of Elizabeth, like those of Edward the Sixth, were curiously associated with the new freedom given to the Scriptures. Lord Bacon relates this incident: "On the morrow of her coronation, it being the custom to release prisoners at the inauguration of a prince, one of her courtiers besought her with a loud voice: That now this good time there might be four or five principal prisoners more released; there were the four Evangelists and the Apostle St. Paul, who had long been shut up in an unknown tongue, as it were in prison, so that they could not converse with the common people."

<small>The release of all the Versions. The greater popularity of the Genevan.</small>

The freedom that followed—and it was now for ever—came alike to all the Versions then in existence; but the Genevan had more than liberty; it had popularity. It was so expressly constructed for the people, and marked such an era of progress on this account that it distanced every other in their affections, and became the household Bible of England. The Great Bible was left far behind. It was restored to the churches for public reading, but the Genevan was read at the hearth-stone. There it remained a favorite for seventy-five years, and became the Bible of the great Puritan party.

THE BISHOPS' BIBLE.

One generous and fearless idea prevailed at this time which it were well if something like it prevailed now. *No official intolerance, as yet, of many versions.* There was no popular uneasiness about the appearance of many versions, and no official determination to make one fixed and unvarying standard, in English, represent the ancient tongues; but there was a tendency to make the last Version better than any former one. Tyndale's and Coverdale's translations and the Great Bible continued to be published. No less than forty editions of them were printed and circulating all through Elizabeth's and James's reign, and ninety of the Genevan.*

Besides these there were several individual Versions; the one already *Liberal policy of archbishop Parker.* noticed by Taverner, and another by Lawrence Tomson, based on the Genevan, and which was very popular. An instance of this want of solicitude on account of such a diversity of

* Anderson. Annals of Eng. Bib. ii. 353.

translations, and how little it entered the mind of the fathers of the English reformation that such could have any effect in undermining the faith of the people—a misgiving strangely prevalent now—is furnished by no less an eminent personage than Cranmer's own successor[*] in the See of Canterbury, archbishop Parker. Even while his thoughts were intent on producing still another Version that should be superior to the Genevan, he used his influence with the authorities to have the Genevan printed in England. (It had been printed all along on the continent.) In his letter to Cecil, he says, That to encourage the Genevan would "nothing hinder, but rather do much good to have diversity of translations and readings."[†] Like Coverdale he felt the contributory power of many minds, and the endless opportunity for improvements and new developments which lay in so great an undertaking. And this it

---

[*] Immediate successor, if we omit the Roman Catholic Reginald Pole.

[†] Plumptre. Smith's Bib. Dict. iii. 1674.

was which urged him on to make even another attempt, in the hope of reaching a more perfect Version still. Never at any time, in this or the succeeding period, did either the people or their leaders dream of attaining a final and unchangeable completeness. The work was always issued like one that might still be improved, and seldom, if ever, were the printers given the book to be set up again without retouches more or less numerous.

It was in this spirit that the English Church made its new endeavor to issue even a better Version than the Genevan, and to resurrect the Great Bible in another big folio, that should again be placed on the lecterns in the cathedrals and churches, and, it was hoped, find also, in a smaller form, an equally popular place on the family table. It was high time that this was done, for the ecclesiastical Great Bible was suffering by comparison with the household Genevan. So the archbishop started on his enterprise in the same direction as Cranmer had before him. *His project of a new Version.*

He laid his plans before the bishops and other learned men. This was in 1563. Like Cranmer he distributed the Bible in parcels among them to receive their corrections and suggestions, after which the fragments were to be returned to him for final revision and publication. Unlike Cranmer he was met with quick and generous encouragement, and after five years' labor, what was known as the "Bishops' Bible" was published by him in a magnificent volume. It incorporated many of the renderings of the Genevan Bible. Four years after, in 1572, another edition was issued, still further revised, especially in the New Testament. So delighted was archbishop Parker with his work that when the volume was finished he uttered the exclamation of Simeon as he took the Christ-child in his arms, "Now lettest Thou Thy servant depart in peace, for mine eyes have seen Thy salvation!"*

<small>Its successful issue, but no assumption of finality for it.</small>

And yet the same wise consciousness of incompleteness comes out

---

* Eng. Hexapla, 42.

in the Preface of the revisers. "There be yet in the Gospels," they say, "very many dark places which without all doubt to posterity shall be made much more open. For why should we despair herein, seeing the Gospel was delivered to this intent that it might be utterly understood of us, yea, to the very inch? Wherefore * * * who can doubt but that such things as remain yet unknown in the Gospel shall be hereafter made open to the later wits of our posterity, to their clear understanding?" "They felt then," says Westcott, "that their labor was provisional, and that the Spirit had yet further lessons in His Word to teach to later ages."*

The whole influence of the church was put forth to make this the Bible of universal use, but the whole preference of the people still continued for the Genevan. The one was the official Version, and the other the popular Version, and both were quite

The rivalry of the Versions.

*Hist. Eng. Bib. 184.

abreast in the race of merit, if not in that of acceptance.

But now we shall come to that other and final endeavor, which took up the Bishops' Bible and revised it so well and so thoroughly that after a long run through a generation or two, the Genevan gave up the race, and retired to its present place as a Version gone out of use. This renewed official attempt was that which produced our present Bible.

IV.

THE PRESENT BIBLE.

Its Formation.—Its General Excellence.—Points of Revision and Improvement.

OUR present Bible is, in the order of its generations since Tyndale, a seventh son. It would seem to have taken its patent of nobility by virtue of that long descent through the most heroic period of the church, and to have earned its title of "The Authorized," because it inherited so many of the excellencies of its ancestors, and produced so many of its own.

The two rival Versions, "the Genevan" and "the Bishops'," con- *Neither the Genevan Version nor the Bishops' satisfactory.* tinued to occupy the realm, the one mostly in the homes, the other mostly in the churches, for a little more than thirty years after the date of the latter's attempt to get the supreme place in the affections of the public. But the Bibles of the Puritans were four times more numerous than the others. Nevertheless neither version was satisfactory to scholars. "Grave fault was found with both." No attempt, however, was made during the remainder of Elizabeth's long reign to produce another; but when James the First ascended the throne the great undertaking which resulted in our present Bible had a most unexpected and sudden birth.

James I. The conflict of the Church party and the Puritan party. James, like Henry the Eighth, a theological monarch, quite deeply read in divinity and proud of considerable ability in it, but at the opposite pole from Henry in being a Presbyterian, came down from Scotland to ascend the throne of England. The two parties of the church were full of agitation; the churchmen dreading what one of them called the coming "Scotch mist," the Puritans confident that a new era was opening favorable to themselves. Both parties sent messengers to meet the king in his progress. The Puritans even burdened their messenger with a bulky petition, signed by seven hundred and fifty clergymen. But the king had learned a lesson or two in the Kirk of Scotland, and was wary of the Puritans. He received the dean of Canterbury, the messenger of the archbishop of Canterbury, graciously, but he issued a proclamation against any more Puritan petitions. It was evident that he intended to maintain the established order of the Church of England, and not accommodate it to the ideas of the powerful party within its borders. The Puritans were especially discontented with the Prayer-Book, and complained of the corrupt translation of the passages of Scripture contained in it, all of which, it will be remembered, were taken from Cranmer's Great Bible and the Bishops' Bible. So the gathering struggle of the adherents of the Genevan Bible with those of the Church Bible, came to an issue in the field of the common liturgy. The Prayer-Book was the battle-ground, and the present Version was the result of the battle; and this result came about, not by the victory of one side and the defeat of the other, but by the unexpected development of a new event, which, like a banner in the sky, diverted the attention of both combatants.

The Hampton Court Conference. This is the singular history. The Puritan clergy asked for a conference with the king and the bishops, at which certain of their representatives should discuss in the royal presence, and with the bishops, the differences which then divided the church. The request was granted. But a frightful plague broke out in London, and the matter had to be postponed for awhile. The king retired to the palace of Hampton Court, a royal abode picturesquely situated some distance up the Thames, and which had been the splendid gift of cardinal Wolsey to king Henry the Eighth. It was within these once alien precincts that the project of the Authorized Version was to be born, for the conference was called together here. King James presided, with much parade of oratory and learning, but listening to the debates with interest and alert intelligence. Nine bishops, six deans, and one archdeacon were present. The bishops were arrayed in their episcopal robes, as when they sat in the House of Lords; the other divines wore the scarlet gowns, customary to doctors of divinity. But the four representatives of the Puritans departed so far from the clerical costume, respectful to the occasion, as to appear in "such gowns as were then commonly worn by Turkey merchants, cloth gowns trimmed with fur."* It was a symbol of their radicalism, and contempt of the church order and tradition. Besides these twenty, there were present some members of the Privy Council, five ecclesiastical lawyers, among whom sat a Scotch Presbyterian minister, "the solitary dissenter." Such was the celebrated Hampton Court Conference. Three days were spent in discussion, but with little result so far as any of the matters, "amiss in the church," pre-

* Blunt. Plain Account of the Eng. Bible, 73.

viously arranged for discussion, were concerned. The controversy raged chiefly around the revision of the Prayer-Book, but with no effect except to bring about "a few verbal changes of no importance whatever." The complaints by the Puritans of the use of the then authorized Bible in the Prayer-Book, brought the debate to a point where both sides, to their surprise, perhaps, came to a sudden agreement. Dr. John Reynolds, President of Corpus Christi College, Oxford, the leader of the Puritan four, "moved his majesty that there might be a new translation of the Bible, because those which were allowed in the reign of Henry the Eighth and Edward the Sixth were corrupt, and not answerable to the truth of the original." It was a motion and a necessity which had been apparently but little considered by these readers of the "Genevan Version," for the alleged corruptions of the "Bishops' Bible," when they named them, were so few and trivial as not to merit discussion. The proposition was met characteristi-

A new Version proposed.

cally by the bishops, with indifference and timid conservatism, the Bishop of London probably giving utterance to the sentiment of the others, by exclaiming, "If every man's humor should be followed, there would be no end of translating." But the king, not yet such a bigoted churchman as to let his common sense be hampered, and at least enough of a Puritan, through his Presbyterian education, to have a ready instinct for progress, with a quick intelligence caught at the idea, and it is owing to him that it did not evaporate with Dr. Reynolds's breath.

"He sketched out in a moment," says Blunt, "an idea of the way in which the work should be undertaken."* *The king favors the undertaking.* He disliked the Genevan Version, because some of its notes were not favorable to king-craft. As to the Bishops' Bible it was confessedly imperfect, and the Great Bible still continued to be read in some of the churches. So there was a want of uniformity, as well, even in the

* Plain Account 75.

Authorized Bible of the church. "His highness," the record says, "wished that some special pains should be taken in that behalf for one uniform translation, and this to be done by the best learned in both the universities; after them to be revised by the bishops and the chief learned of the church; from them to be presented to the Privy Council; and, lastly, to be ratified by his royal authority. And so this whole church to be bound upon it, and none other." He added, on the suggestion of the bishop of London, "that no marginal notes should be added" like those "annexed to the Geneva translation."

The conference broke up; the Puritans having been driven from point to point by the onsets of the bishops, and failing at last in all, except in the result of this one immature proposition, which did make a lodgment in the royal, if not in the episcopal mind, and was destined shortly, by the royal influence, to take the magnificent shape in which it afterward appeared.

During the next five months the king was busy with his councillors in selecting those to whom the new translation was to be committed, organizing the "companies" into which they were to be divided, arranging the method of the work, and laying down the principles upon which it should be executed. Fifty-four distinguished scholars were fixed upon, and, by command of the king, Bancroft bishop of London communicated with each of them, "informing them that it was the king's pleasure that they should begin their work immediately." One very practical suggestion, of a material nature, was acted upon in the month following. In order to insure the pecuniary support of the translators during the long labor now assigned them, some of whom had to give up their regular church or professional engagements, the archbishops and bishops were enjoined to keep in reserve whatever gifts of position and emolument were in their hands, or under their influence, for those who were insufficiently

The plan of it elaborated.

provided. Contributions of money also were solicited, and other measures suggested to meet the expenses of the undertaking.

<small>Composition of the companies who were to make the revision.</small> The companies were made up with justice and liberality in other respects also. There were as many clergy of the Puritan party appointed as of the Church party: among them Dr. Reynolds, and Dr. Chatterton, one of his fellows at the conference. Laymen, also, of eminent scholarship, were associated with the clergy—and the bishops were enjoined by the king "to inform themselves of all such learned men within their several dioceses, as, having especial skill in the Hebrew and Greek tongues, have taken pains in their private studies of the Scriptures, for the clearing of any obscurities either in the Hebrew or in the Greek, or touching any difficulties or mistakings in the former English translation, which we have now commanded to be thoroughly viewed and amended, and thereupon to write unto them, earnestly charging them, and signifying our pleasure therein,

that they send such their observations * * * to be imparted to the rest of their several companies; that so our said intended translation may have the help and furtherance of all our principal learned men."

Thus the preparations for the undertaking were most elaborate and thorough. All the learning of the kingdom was to be concentrated upon it. And yet it was looked upon by all as still tentative—still only an attempt to reach a greater perfection than any of its predecessors—still a *feeling out* into the future. The Preface claims for it neither the merit of originality nor the intent of finality. As the work was itself derived, so all that was hoped for it was the superior excellence which could not but result after such an amount of care, labor, and scholarly pains had been expended upon it. It was regarded as only one grander step forward than had yet been taken.

The project looked upon as only a new endeavor.

The principles and instructions which were given to guide the

The principles of the new revision.

undertaking are in themselves a foreview of its history, and exhibit the limitations by which it was kept from attaining the perfect ideal even then before some scholarly minds.

It is unnecessary to detail in full these instructions, but the mention of a few will draw attention to the points where it was compelled to fall short.

The first injunction was to make the "Bishops' Bible" the basis of the revision, and to alter it as little as the original would permit. Already had there set in around this, the Authorized Version of that day, something of the reverential feeling which has gathered about the present one, and this injunction was "intended probably to quiet the alarm of those who saw, in the proposal of a new Version, a condemnation of that already existing."* The ecclesiastical words, which Tyndale had neglected, and Coverdale had restored, were to be retained—and so we have "church" instead of "congregation," and "charity"

* Plumptre. Smith's Bib. Dict. iii. 1676.

instead of "love," &c. "When a word hath divers significations," runs the fourth rule, "that to be kept which hath been most commonly used by the most ancient fathers, being agreeable to the propriety of the place, and the analogy of the faith." "This," says Plumptre, "like the former, tends to confound the functions of the preacher and the translator, and substitutes ecclesiastical tradition for philological accuracy." The fifth rule directs "the division of chapters to be altered either not at all, or as little as may be, if necessity so require." On which Plumptre comments: "Here, again, convenience was more in view than truth or accuracy, and the result is that divisions are perpetuated which are manifestly arbitrary and misleading."

The sixth rule enjoined "no marginal notes at all to be affixed, but only for the explanation of the Hebrew or Greek words, which cannot, without some circumlocution, so briefly and fitly be expressed in the text;" on which, among other things, Mr. Plumptre well remarks. "Had an opposite course been adopted, we might have had the tremendous evil of a whole body of exegesis imposed upon the church by authority, reflecting the Calvinism of the synod of Dort, the absolutism of James, the high-flying prelacy of Bancroft."

The remaining portion of the rules sketches the plan of the revision, makes provision for difficulties and for a wider consultation with scholars, if necessary, appoints the directors of the work, and finally names the Versions of Tyndale, Coverdale, Rogers, Cranmer, and Geneva, enjoining that if the renderings of any of them should agree more with the originals than those of the "Bishops' Bible," they should be adopted.

The Revision simultaneously commenced in 1607 at London, Oxford, and Cambridge. The revisers—forty-seven, not fifty-four as appointed—divided into six companies, set to work simultaneously in Westminster, Oxford, and Cambridge, two companies in each place, one engaged on the Old Testament, the other on the New. This was in 1607. The work (which very likely had been already begun in parts) proceeded so noiselessly for the four years to come that we can hardly find anything in contemporary documents or correspondence which will give us an inner glimpse of its progress. The process, we know, was this. The translators being gathered at their three centres, two companies at each centre, every member of a company took the same portion, and translated and amended it by himself. Then all met together, each bringing his own work. After a collation and comparison of renderings a selection was agreed upon, and then a single copy made of the portion as thus revised. Selden, in his "Table Talk," opens to us an inside view at this stage of the proceedings. "That part of the Bible was given to him," he says, "who was most excellent in such a tongue, and then they met together, and one read the translation, the rest holding in their hands some Bible, either of the learned tongues, or French,

<small>The process.</small>

Spanish, Italian, &c.; if they found any fault they spoke; if not, he read on."*

The work of a company being thus far done, the result was sent to the other companies for criticism. If alterations were suggested which were approved, they were adopted at once. If the suggestions were not agreed to, they were referred to a final committee of revisers. This committee, composed of two from each company, met at the close in London. Thus every portion passed through thirteen, and sometimes sixteen, examinations, and, as the substance of every portion was the Bishops' Bible, the process was like a system of natural filtration by which that work was clarified and purified; and a very close system of filtration it proved to be,

---

* These Bibles were, beside those already mentioned, the Douay-Rhemish version (from which many Latinized words were taken), several new Latin Versions which had appeared, the authorized French Bible, put forth by "the Venerable Company of Pastors" at Geneva, an Italian translation just issued (1607) by Diodati, and two Spanish versions.

for never before was any version, on the whole, so colorless or so pure as this which had percolated through such a varied stratification. Filtration, however, can hardly describe the whole process, unless there be included with it a positive element of improvement derived from the different media through which the percolation passed, in which case the living water, though not less colorless, may be said to have now issued forth with additional virtue as a healing power.

The year 1611 saw our present Bible published, in a large black-letter folio, by the committee of final revision. *Published after the labor of four years.* It had much in its favor, already, to commend it to the public. It came with the whole influence of the throne, with the prestige of contemporary scholarship, and finally with the great advantage of a general adoption by the Established Church, for the publication of the "Bishops' Bible" ceased when it was issued.*

---

* Though its adoption was general, yet in some churches the "Bishops' Bible" was not displaced by it for a long

But to none of these advantages does there seem to have been given any undue prominence or pressure by the authorities. The work was left with the greatest confidence to make its own way among the people, and to distance if it could by its own intrinsic merits all competitors. The following remarkable statement is made by Mr. Westcott: "No evidence has yet been produced to show that the version was ever publicly sanctioned by Convocation or by Parliament, or by the Privy Council, or by the king. It gained its currency partly, it may have been by the weight of the king's name, partly by the personal authority of the prelates and scholars who had been engaged upon it, but still more by its own intrinsic superiority over all its rivals."*

How it came to be the "Authorized Version." The Genevan Bible continued to be printed and continued to be read (in a way that will shortly be told), time. Ten years after its publication we find Bishop Andrews, one of its leading revisers, taking the texts of his sermons from the "Bishops' Bible."

* Hist. Eng. Bib. 158.

but, by the middle of the century, after a competition of fifty years, it had gradually gone out of use, and thus the " Authorized Version" of the present day proves to have taken its own place not by royal decree, but by the choice of the people: "Authorized" because preferred and accepted by them. It marks a curious revolution in a single century, for, scarcely one hundred years before, Tyndale and his Version made on behalf of the people, could not get even the ear of the king, much less his license, and now the matter was so completely turned the other way, that the king, having originated and elaborated a most perfect revision, appeals to the will and leaves it all to the consent of the people. What a change too, and what a consummation since Wycliffe's day! Mr. Westcott thus eloquently concludes his own history: " Whatever else may be thought of the story which has been thus imperfectly told, enough has been said to show that the history of the English Scriptures is, as was remarked by anticipation, unique. The other great vernacular versions of Europe are the works of single men, definitely stamped with their impress and bearing their names. A German writer somewhat contemptuously remarks that it took nearly a century to accomplish in England the work which Luther achieved in the fraction of a single lifetime. The reproach is exactly our glory. Our Version is the work of a church and not of a man, or rather it is a growth and not a work. Countless external influences, independent of the actual translators, contributed to mould it; and when it was fashioned the Christian instinct of the nation, touched, as we believe, by the Spirit of God, decided on its authority. But at the same time, as if to save us from that worship of the letter, which is the counterfeit of true and implicit devotion to the sacred text, the same original words are offered to us in other forms in our Prayer-Book, and thus the sanction of use is distinguished from the claims to finality. Our Bible, in virtue of its past, is capable of admitting revision, if need be, without violating its history. As it gathered into itself, during the hundred years in which it was forming, the treasures of manifold labors, so it still has the same assimilative power of life."*

The history of the immediate outset of the "King's Bible," as it was called, is a singular one, and shows that this universal authorization, though it came at last, was long delayed—delayed not by a want of appreciation, but by party strife. Five editions of it were rapidly issued, and were an earnest of the success which belonged to it, but the times were in tumult with the Puritan excitement, which was on the increase. There was a rampant use and abuse of the Genevan Bible for the next fifty years, under the influence of this excitement, which, as in all such cases, kept the calmer and greater power biding its time in the background. The irresponsible issue of the Puritan Bible by the printers, in countless numbers, and in all forms and sizes,

<small>The strange fate and experience of the Genevan Bible before it went out of use.</small>

* Hist. Eng. Bib. 370.

under a wild and often unprincipled demand, brought into it errors of the most serious description. Many of these were purposely introduced, either in a spirit of mischief to create confusion, and with malignant intent against a doctrine of the church, or with the design to advance and sustain some half-fledged sectarian creed. "The important negative" was, in one edition, left out of the seventh commandment, and out of many another passage also, to the complete perversion of both precept and doctrine. Sometimes whole texts were left out. The learned Usher is described as hastening one day to preach at "Paul's Cross," and stoping on the way at a bookseller's to purchase a Bible, but "when he came to look for his text, he found to his astonishment and horror" that the verse had been omitted! In one Bible six thousand errors were discovered. In another, three thousand six hundred. The great Selden used to get up in the Puritan "Assembly of Divines," where the most ignorant discussions often prevailed, sustained by these diminutive Bibles, which every one was ready to pull out and quote in "chapter and verse," and say, "Perhaps in your little pocket Bible with gilt leaves the translation may be so, but the Greek or the Hebrew signifies this." "While these transactions were occurring," says D'Israeli,* "it appears that the authentic translation of the Bible, such as we now have it, by the learned translators in James the First's time, was suffered to lie neglected. The copies of the original manuscript were in the possession of two of the king's printers, who, from cowardice, consent, and connivance, suppressed the publication; considering that a Bible full of errata, and often, probably, accommodated to the notions of certain sectarists, was more valuable than one authenticated by the hierarchy! Such was the state of the English Bible till 1660!"

But the period of Puritan domination came to an end, and then the "King's Bible" took all the more *The final acceptance and permanence of the Authorized Version.*

* Curiosities of Literature, iv. 354.

triumphant place, like a rock which had been only washed over and submerged, but not displaced, by the waves of fanaticism. It grew rapidly in popular esteem. Still, not until the reign of Queen Anne, nearly one hundred years after its first appearance, did it take that very exalted position which has been accorded to it ever since. Then "the tide of glowing panegyric set in," says Plumptre. "It would be easy to put together a long *catena* of praises stretching from that time to the present. With many, of course, this has been only the routine repetition of a traditional boast. 'Our unrivalled translation,' and 'our incomparable Liturgy' have been, equally, phrases of course. But there have been witnesses of a far higher weight. In proportion as the English of the eighteenth century was infected with a Latinized or Gallicised style, did those who had a purer taste look with reverence to the strength and purity of a better time as represented by the Authorized Version.

* * * Each half-century has naturally added to the prestige of these merits."*

It is these literary excellences which constitute now its strength and unattainable perfection. And they were the work of time—the work, also, of its extraordinary evolution out of a remarkable opportunity in the history of our language, and its passage through as remarkable an experience. No amount of skill or ingenuity could produce such another style, so exquisitely simple and so curiously interwoven with the oriental idiom of the originals. The story of its gradual production is its best eulogy. It contains the wealth of seven antecedent Versions, and of as many contemporary Versions in other tongues. It took the savor of antiquity from the moment Tyndale touched it, and it always leaned back into the past at any subsequent revision. At no time was it other than olden and oriental in its modes and forms of phraseology, and therefore,

margin note: The elements of its essential perfection and permanency.

---

* Smith's Bib. Dict. iii. 1678.

as a representative of the originals, themselves so far in the past, this one element of it as a translation is of unspeakable value. Whatever may be done with it hereafter, this feature will be most jealously guarded, and will never be permitted to depart from it.

The elements of its present imperfection and improvement. But time has wrought a change in it, and around it, as in all other things, a change which does not touch this its inestimable peculiarity, but which has made more conspicuous certain defects in its structure, that were not so apparent in its own age, and were only noticed here and there by learned men in the early course of its progress.

A still corrupt original text. Progress of textual criticism. To recur to the obvious analogy which has prevailed through this history: after two hundred and sixty years have passed, it has been found necessary to re-examine and repair the ancient building of the Authorized Version. A new set of workmen have been down in the crypt of the original languages, and while they have found the massive walls and vaulted archways generally secure, yet, in the New Testament especially, they have discovered so many minor imperfections in this textual foundation which Erasmus, Ximenes, Stephens, and Beza laid, that its solidity is seriously affected. These new workmen upon the deep-laid foundations, and in a darkness which has all along removed them from popular sight and appreciation, are almost too many, now, to mention in detail. We must content ourselves with the names of the master-workmen. John Mill began at it before the seventeenth century was out. Then Bengel and Wetstein, in Germany, devoted themselves to it in the first part of the eighteenth century. In this the nineteenth century, Griesbach, Scholtz, Lachman, and Tischendorf, all Germans, and Tregelles, Wordsworth, Ellicott, and Alford, all Englishmen, have labored so magnificently, that even the unscholarly mind has sometimes taken a rush-light and gone down into the crypt to curiously view their stupendous achievements in the way of emendation, and the astonishing contributions to the strength of the original walls which several of them have made in their discovery of forgotten stones, chiselled for this very work, but left in the quarry until now.*

<small>The effect of this and of time on the English text also.</small>

And time has had its inevitable way, also, with the English walls above. Many a competent architect-translator has watched them with anxiety for many years. Here and there a crack has come from the want of perfect solidity below. In many places the imperfect masonry of the early builders has begun to expose itself. And, everywhere, also, not deeply, not essentially, but still importantly, the sure corrosion of years is manifest in words crumbling away from their primitive import, scaling off from their original force and beauty, like the stones in the quadrangles of the Oxford colleges, and

---

* The signalizing of the "Thousandth English Tauchnitz" by the issue of the New Testament under the direction of Tischendorf, showing the various readings of the three oldest MSS., is an indication of the popular interest in this province of inquiry.

the fronts of old cathedrals, and making one apprehensive, if not of ultimate destruction, at least of the loss of much present strength and meaning, should nothing be done to arrest decay. If we add to this the existence of some deformities and excrescences, unnecessarily suffered to appear in the too literal rendition of an age grosser in taste than this, allowed in it like the coarse grotesques of ancient architecture, we sum up the whole of those serious imperfections which have given rise to the present inevitable, and we may say, irresistible movement toward a new revision of the Scriptures.

Still one other want has been developed by time, in the progress of intellect and inquiry. *A notable deficiency.* Hitherto the English Bible, through one great omission in its making up, has failed to convey its whole suggestion, and to adapt itself to the human life of to-day, or rather, to speak more correctly, the human life of to-day has not been drawn by it back into the ages of its original inspiration, and made to live over again the experience out of which it grew. The Version implies a modern consciousness throughout, and resembles, in its absence of allusion to the ancient and Eastern types of life, that celebrated picture by Paul Veronese, of the marriage at Cana of Galilee, now in the Louvre, where a great Venetian feast-table is portrayed on a huge canvas, crowded around by lords and ladies in the rich and gorgeous costumes worn by the contemporaries of the painter. The *circumstances* under which the original outwardly grew, and under which the successive parts of its great interior history unfolded itself, ought to be made actual and vivid to the modern imagination. This is a matter, not so much of translation as of restoration. Accompanying the process which, like translation, transports, so to speak, the ancient work into the present time, there ought to be a process of revivification or resuscitation by which the mind and situation of the past should be made entirely familiar to the consciousness of the present day. The Bible can never be intelligently read, and the full proportion and relation of its parts can never be properly apprehended, nor can its whole living, breathing, every-day humanity be realized, unless the translation is supplemented by a system of dense and graphic notes (not "comments") which shall revive the manners, the customs, the scenes, the institutions, the ideas, the traditions, and even the superstitions which prevailed at the time its several scrolls were written. The Book must not only be translated forward into the age of the reader, but the reader himself must also be translated backward into the ages of the Book. His mind and heart must be after a manner orientalized, before he can become competent to understand with full intelligence the peculiar methods and allusions of oriental speech and life.

The Genevan version, among its other wise provisions, moved somewhat in this direction, by introducing into one of its later editions a Bible Dic- *The need of archæological notes to revive its ancient circumstances.*

tionary. But the present need of the English Bible, a need never so manifest before, is a full accompaniment of archæological foot-notes, drawn from the immense treasury of such knowledge which has accumulated in recent years. The very fact that such a number of scholars have been lately so active in seeking and acquiring knowledge of this character is an indication of the mental demand of the age, and ought to be more than a hint to the next editors of the English Scriptures. If this is not to be a feature of the coming Bible, its narratives, its prophecies, and its teachings will continue to be, as they have been, without a background or an atmosphere. Its historic scenes will still appear like the pictures of Chinese art, without perspective, piled one on the top of the other, and the living words of Christ and of His apostles will come to the reader without the vital air, as it were, on which they were spoken, and by which only they could have been *then* truly articulated and therefore be *now* truly apprehended.

The following are the points or occasions of incompleteness which affect our present Bible, and which were inevitable, either in the age of its production, or in the subsequent passage of years: *First:* the admitted imperfection of the original texts—particularly the Greek text—this having been made especially manifest by the late discovery and collation of manuscripts of much greater age and authority; *second:* the comparatively insufficient knowledge of the original languages on the part of the translators, especially in some of the niceties of grammar and philology : *third:* the insensible lapse of our own language, and the obsolete and obsolescent character, therefore, of many of our words, by which the meaning they had once, has gone out of them, and by which they have become assigned to other and narrower uses and associations; *fourth:* the lack of brief philological (not theological), annotations, critically developing all the subtilties couched in a word or phrase of the original, and also of a full marginal "*variorum*,"

Five points of incompleteness.

or renderings of different hands, by the combination of which the whole force and spirit of the original should be thrown out, like an odor, whenever the English expression adopted in the text might prove to be inadequate without a resort to circumlocution; *fifth:* the lack also of archæological notes which would restore, as far as possible, the occasion of the original composition and the contemporary circumstances of each book, and, in some cases, part of a book.

<small>Seven errors of judgment.</small> To these negative points of incompleteness may be added these positive errors of judgment: *first,* in the division of the books into chapters,* and the chap-

---

* The translators are not responsible for the division into chapters, but for the adoption of it. "It derived its origin from Cardinal Caro, who lived in the twelfth century." See *Campbell's Translation of the Gospels,* I. 492.

"There are several instances in which the sense is injured, if not destroyed, by an improper division. Very often the chapter breaks off in the midst of a narrative, and if the reader stops because the chapter ends, he loses the connection. Sometimes the break is altogether in the wrong place, and separates two sentences which must be

ters into verses,* in places where the sense of a passage is interrupted by the division; *second,* in the breaking up of the paragraphs into verses instead of keeping the figures on the margin to facilitate reference merely; *third,* in the introduction of the chapter-headings, by

taken together in order to be understood."—*Eadie's Bibl. Encyclopedia.*

"In each of the following sixteen passages, the connection between the end of one chapter, and the beginning of the other, is so intimate as to render the chapter division extremely unsuitable: 1 Sam. ix. x.; Eccles. xi. xii.; Song iv. v.; Isa. lii. liii.; Ezek. i. ii.; Amos i. ii.; Jonah i. ii.; iii. iv.; Mark viii. ix.; John xviii. xix.; Acts iv. v.; xxi. xxii.; 2 Cor. iv. v.; Gal. iv. v.; Eph. v. vi.; Heb. iii. iv. Such are a *few* specimens of the extreme inaccuracy with which the text of Scripture is divided."—*Plea for a New Engl. Version of the Scriptures, by a Licentiate of the Church of Scotland,* 199.

* "The following are a few of many passages in which the versification is extremely inaccurate: Exod. xx. 5, 6; 9, 10; Deut. xxxiv. 1, 2, 3; 10, 11, 12; Isa. lxii. 6, 7; John iii. 14, 15; Rom. viii. 33, 34; 1 Cor. iii. 22, 23; vi. 19, 20; vii. 29, 30, 31; Gal. v. 19, 20, 21; 22, 23; Eph. i. 15, 16; 2 Tim. iii. 16, 17; Heb. i. 1, 2; 1 Pet

which an interpretative gloss or commentary is often made, as in the case of the Canticles, Psalms, and Prophets, to anticipate the reading of a chapter; *fourth*, the introduction of an excessive amount of italicised expressions, originally intended to clear the meaning, but which in some cases affect the sense;* *fifth*, a want of uniformity in proper names, by which the personages of the Old Testament are hardly recognisable in the New, and the connection of the two histories is almost broken apart;†

i. 3, 4, 5. In each of these sixteen passages the former verse ends and the latter begins in the midst of a sentence." *Ib.* 197.

* This was done after 1611. Great errors crept into the text, and it had to be revised. This revision was made by Dr. Scattergood in 1683 and by Dr. Blayney in 1769. The latter revised the punctuation, examined and corrected the italics, introducing them more frequently than was necessary, altered the summaries of the chapters and running titles, corrected errors in chronology, and greatly increased the number of the marginal references.

† *E. g.* Elias for Elijah, Eliseus for Elisha, Noe for Noah, Cis for Kish, Jesus for Joshua, and so on.

sixth, errors in punctuation, and especially the want of quotation marks, by which the frequent citations of the Old Testament Scriptures are made almost unapparent, and the individual speeches which appear in both Testaments are allowed to blend themselves with the comments and context of the writer;* and *seventh*—a matter of translation—the indelicacy of many passages, especially in the Old Testament, which even a fidelity to the original does not make necessary, and which would only have appeared in an age when literary and social taste was grosser than in this.

There were two disadvantages under which the translators labored, and which accounts for much of the inadequacy of their Version. In the first place

(marginal note: The translators' imperfect knowledge of oriental antiquities, and of Greek and Hebrew.)

---

* In some cases it will not be easy to satisfy all readers that the marks of quotation are inserted in the right place and properly indicate the termination of a reported utterance, and the beginning of the reporter's comment, but in such instances the doubt ought to be honestly stated and the reader be left to form his own opinion.

they were not as well informed as we are now in the manners, customs, traditions, ideas, and general mind of the East; and in the next place, instead of learning Greek and Hebrew, as we do, through English grammars and lexicons, and other philological aids, they learned the Greek through the Latin, which was almost a vernacular language to them, but a very coarse medium through which to study the subtilest tongue on earth. The Greek has a much closer affinity to the English than to the Latin. But reading it with these Latin lenses, the translators often failed to render the true force of tenses, cases, prepositions, and articles, and so we have lost some of the finer shades which give emphasis and vividness to the original—not to speak of being sometimes more seriously misled. As to the Hebrew, there was another limitation, quite as unfortunate. In the strict line of Old Testament Hebrew, there were probably as great scholars then as now. Broughton, (one of the projectors though not one of the translators of the present Bible, and a severe critic of the version when finished,) could speak it like his native tongue. But it was learned at that time in the close tradition of the Rabbins, and not with the wider illustration of the cognate Semitic languages which have been opened by scholars since.

Mr. Blunt, an opponent of revision, says of the present Bible: *The movement to revision a demand of the age.* "The plain man may use it with a firm confidence that he is using that which will give him substantially true impressions of what has come down to us under the name of Holy Scripture."* This is no more than any one is prepared to say of "Our dear old English Bible." For a "plain" unlearned Christian, who may devotionally read it, it is all-sufficient. It does convey "substantially" all of God's truth, and in the sweetest and richest of rhythmical language. But the movement to revision, which to-day has become so earnest and serious as to engage the attention of such a large number of English bishops—the most conser-

---

* Plain Account, 97.

vative of all men—and which has come at last to them after the subject has been agitated so many years, is not made in the interest of "plain," simple minds, but of a great, thinking, questioning, scrutinizing age; it is made in the interest of honesty and truth; it is made because "the people" who have "authorized" the present Version, desire it and demand it. This is an age when the people, more than ever, think and read for themselves, and with a culture and intelligence never known before. Their reasonable wish is that their Bible should come to them with no darkness, nor even dimness upon any part of it, that it should represent the original to the utmost, and that every facility should be given them for arriving at the most perfect knowledge of what is conveyed to them in this word of God. The advanced character of the age, therefore, is in itself an argument for a new advance also in the English Bible.

<small>The historical argument for revision.</small> And for that Bible to advance is only a part of its genius, and in the

order of its history. As we have seen, it is, in itself, the consummate result of repeated revisions. Purvey revised Wycliffe,* Tyndale revised himself many times, and very probably caught much of his simplicity of style and ancient flavor from both Wycliffe and Purvey. Coverdale revised Tyndale, Rogers revised Tyndale and Coverdale, the Bible of Cromwell was a revision of the Bible of Rogers, the Bible of Cranmer was a revision of the Bible of Cromwell, the Bible of Geneva was a revision of the Bible of Cranmer, the Bible of the Bishops was a revision of the Bible of Cranmer and of Geneva, and, finally, the Bible of king James was a revision of the Bible of the Bishops, with the seven antecedent Bibles open around his translators, expressly to contribute each its strength to the mighty work which the necessity and the spirit of that age had inspired. In the momentum of such a history, in the impetus of such an experience, it can be

---

* Perhaps, as Mr. Blunt says, Wycliffe's Version was a revision of the previous Saxon and Norman Versions.

nothing new or strange to see the Scriptures ushered even once more upon another critical period, into a new era, when still another revision shall revive the waning interest, and excite the latent enthusiasm of minds which have never yet dreamed of or realized the depth of their divinity and the breadth of their humanity, as a message from God to man. We must have a care of that tendency in us to the official "black-letter,"* which would retain the Bible in its present shape, because that shape is traditional and venerable, even at the risk of alienating those who would otherwise read it; and we must learn, at such a time as this, to take hold of the mind of the age in the wise spirit of the more popular "roman letter," and make it an attractive, intelligible, powerful, and penetrating word direct to the hearts and the homes of the people. The church would reverse the whole of her history, and forget the lessons of her experience, if she should act now with any conservative

* See p. 133.

reserve or timidity in giving to the world just that Bible which the world needs. In the spirit of Wycliffe let her think of the Bible as expressly *for the people*. In the spirit of Tyndale let her make it colorless of any church preconception, and convey absolutely what the original conveys. In the spirit of Coverdale, let her gather the rich marginal illustration of many translators around the English text. In the spirit of Cranmer, let her issue it as from the church, with conscientiousness, with dignity, and with authority. In the spirit of Geneva, let her issue it without official vesture, as a thing of humanity as well as divinity, with the contributed power of a scholarship outside the church, and with the lamp of antiquity in its hand to illumine the darkness behind the page and behind the reader's eye. In the spirit of the Bishops, let her publish it in the hope that it may exceed in excellence its predecessor and competitor, and yet in generous confidence, let her give all its rivals room. And, finally, in the spirit of king James and of the church in his time, let her work be so carefully, so elaborately, so courageously complete, both as a Version and as an arrangement, that she may commit it without reserve to the intelligent judgment of the age, and trust to its being "authorized" again by the unanimous preference, both of the church and of the people, through the compelling power of its own perfection.

<small>No extensive alteration designed.</small> The delineation of all this cumulative force, which ought to go into the next Version, may very possibly give the reader the idea of extensive alteration: such as would almost destroy the identity of the Bible and make it look like a new book. This is not designed by the present movement in the Church of England, and it can never take place. The present Version is too generally complete and satisfactory already, to admit of any change which would affect its familiar and reverend form. The revision now going on, is no more than a process of preservation and renovation, like that which may be, and

often is, applied to an ancient work of art. The great unfinished picture of an old master, the lines of whose genius no after-hand would dare to touch, may yet be growing dimmer and dimmer in the lapse of time, its colors may be gradually fading out, the distinctness of its purpose may be much impaired, the crust of time may be gathering over it, and the tooth of time be eating away the very canvas on which the precious work is laid. It becomes then a work of duty both to the painter and to the world, that some skilful hand should remove the dust of years and bring out the colors anew in their olden beauty; that some pencil, allied in genius with its author, should strike in the unfinished lines, and so complete the work; and that by the process of another and newer art, the work on the perishable canvas should be transferred to the imperishable stones of the mosaic. In like manner this act of revision is only a cleaning and retouching and completing of the ancient picture, which portrays the history of our faith, and it is an act of rescuing it from the ravages of time by transferring it to the more permanent conditions of the present day. And these permanent conditions of the present day are the open-eyed scrutiny with which the age approaches everything, and the open-hearted honesty with which everything approaches the age.

The fiery test of adverse criticism has revealed the truth of the original. The fires of verbal criticism have burned around the original text, and the flames of historical criticism have risen around the books of Scripture, but they have burned and raged only to reveal the pure asbestos of the divine origin and character belonging to both.

So a thorough and fearless revision will insure the permanency of the work, and unfold its full power to the age. And in like manner this new presentment of them in our daily tongue, must be so true, so clear, that criticism can no longer criticise, that the vision of things divine shall be no longer dim, that their inspiration shall be no longer doubtful: the whole Bible, whether as history, or prophecy, or psalmody, whether as the life of Christ, or as the opening story of the early church, to be so vivid in every part, so richly circumstanced throughout, and so duly proportioned in the measure of the importance belonging to every book, that the Truth shall come out in a spirit stronger than the letter, and like the sun, which in its rising and in its setting gives a glory to the clouds that is not their own, fill these human words of man's contrivance with the splendors of a meaning which none but heavenly light could have painted on them.

Christianity can rely on itself, and on its own consistency with itself, for its best evidence and best credential. Let then every veil be lifted from its blessed record, let every occasion of dimness be cleared away, that every eye may see its greatness, and every heart bow down before its power.

This little history has been prepared because the time is ripe for the subject; because the new crisis has come, and because, already, authorized companies of distinguished men are engaged in trying to

Conclusion.

meet it.* We ourselves are passing through just such another period as one of those which gave each time the English Bible a new and better form. We are at a new stage of its

---

* The mode of procedure by the present revisers is modelled on that of their predecessors in King James's time. As the latter took the then official Bible, "the Bishops'," for the basis of their revision, so the former take "The King's Bible" for the basis of the new revision, and seem to go to work with almost too much fear of making even most necessary changes—(at least this is the impression conveyed by Bishop Ellicott's little book). The old church conservatism still lingers in them, and no doubt, on the whole, wisely. Better that they should be slow than too fast, timid rather than rash. They are divided into two companies, instead of six; one engaged on the Old Testament and the other on the New. Their number is not so great as in the former revision, but vast treasures of scholarship have accumulated since then, which are entirely in their possession. One significant element of the new movement is the union with it, by invitation, of eminent scholars outside the English Church. For a full account of the character and principles of the movement see *Bishop Ellicott " On the Revision of the English New Testament," London,* 1870.

history. The Holy Book is to take another step onward. It is to leave behind the imperfections of its former construction, and to assume that additional completeness which will adapt it to the necessities of a new and remarkable age. Surely, this alone were occasion enough for such a delineation of the successive epochs of its development, as has now been so imperfectly performed.

But even if there were no such issue at hand, the account of its strange and eventful history could not but add a tenfold interest to it, and reverence for it as it is. It lives among us the venerable relic of a terrible and stirring age. It came into being amid persecution and exile. It was sprinkled with the ashes of the stake, and the blood of the block. It was trampled under foot by one king, but it became the royal diadem of another. It was tried as silver is tried, and as gold refined seven times in the fire, for in seven successive crucibles of intellect, saintliness, and scholarship, was it gradually purged of its dross. It was commenced in the secret closet of a lone translator, hidden amid the obscurities of a Continental town; it was finished in the open chamber of a congress of scholars in the heart of the metropolis of England. At the first in journeyings often, in perils of waters, in perils of robbers, in perils of its own countrymen, in weariness and painfulness, in watchings often, in hunger and thirst, in fastings often, in cold and nakedness, it reached repose at last in the courts of princes and governors, in the cloisters of universities and cathedrals, in the hearths and homes of the millions of a nation. It has appeared in the agitations of the state, and it has felt all the vicissitudes of the church. The most critical century of the church's history is mirrored in its bosom, and all the fluctuations of her doctrine, during her season of trial, have been reflected in the mutations of its language.

The labor expended in these pages will have been well bestowed if they shall have given new interest to this wonderful historic fruit and flower, and furnished a renewed occasion of reverence for that which deserves, by the heroism and singularity of its experience in our native tongue, as well as by the Divinity of its inspiration and authorship in the tongues of men now dead and gone, the title of the "Book of Books."

APPENDIX.

A Note.

IT has not been thought necessary to give a list of the imperfections which originally appeared in the English Version, nor of the others which have since become so conspicuously manifest. Most of them will be found in a sort of tabulated form, and well reasoned for besides, in the "Plea for a new English Version of the Scriptures, by a Licentiate of the Church of Scotland." Many works of like character have appeared of late years, and, in some cases, entire Versions by eminent scholars and philologists. The following celebrated persons are associated with this movement as its advocates, either in their works or by their individual translations: Lowth, Doddridge, Wesley, Campbell, Newcome, Waterland, in days gone by, and, to-day, Trench, Scholefield, Ellicott, Alford, Stanley, Jowett, Conybeare, Howson, and many others.

It may be as well to refer the reader to the following works lately published, containing suggestions, more or less numerous, for a new revision: Archbishop Trench "On the Authorized Version," and "The Synonyms of the New Testament." Dewes's "Plea for a New Translation of the Scriptures." Scholefield's "Hints for some Improvements in the Authorized Version of the New Testament." Alford's "How to Study the New Testament." "New Testament for English Readers," and "Greek Testament." Francis Trench's "Notes on the New Testament." Bishop Ellicott "On the Revision of the English Version of the New Testament." Lightfoot's "Fresh Revision of the New Testament." A list of the new "Versions" which have lately appeared would fill another page.

The writer ventures to append the following on a point that has seemed to be strangely overlooked by most, though not by all, and, in the overlooking, to involve even so great an inversion as the making the *ethical* element of our religion secondary to the *emotional*.

The Greek words have been printed in English letters also, in order that the subject may be understood by any reader.

The Renderings "Repent Ye" and "Repentance" Inadequate and Misleading.

THESE are the great initial, foreshadowing words of the Gospel which meet the reader as he opens his New Testament, at the point where its action begins. In Matt. iii. 12, one of them represents the theme of John the Baptist's preaching, or more properly heralding, "Repent ye!" In Mark i. 4, and Luke iii. 3, the other appears as his theme in connection with a certain practical test and outward symbol, "the baptism of *Repentance*." Further on in Matt. iv. 17, and Mark i. 15, the proclaiming, comprehensive first appears again "when Jesus began to preach," after the voice of John had been hushed in prison: "Repent ye!" Taking the Evangelists thus in harmony the reader finds the keynote and strain of the whole Gospel struck in these words of its earliest announcement. They are in themselves harbingers. But I forget. If he reads the *English* New Testament, with no knowledge of the Greek, he does *not* find the tenor of the whole Gospel anticipated in them, and what is more, he finds no expression in the beginning of John's Gospel which corresponds to them— thus throwing it out of harmony in this particular. If, on the contrary, he reads them in the original, he finds it otherwise; at least so I must understand if I am right in what follows.

The Authorized Version was made to bring the Scriptures to the common people. The learned had them already in the Greek and Hebrew originals, or in Latin Versions. The endeavor was to create an English Standard of revealed truth, so plain as to be understood by Tyndale's "plough-boy" on the one hand, and so exact as to be available for citation by teachers of the truth on the other. The words "Repent ye" and "Repentance" are supposed then to represent the Greek, and to convey the same impression to people now as the original words did to the first readers of the Gospels. We turn then to the common mirrors of speech, in its popular use, to ascertain what the people do really understand by them. Bailey's Etymological Dictionary defines Repentance: "a sorrow for past deeds or omissions." Worcester's Dictionary defines it: "The state of being penitent; sorrow or pain for something done or left undone; penitence; contrition; compunction; remorse." This is its primary signification. A secondary one is then given, taken from the theological books: "Sorrow for sin, such as produces amendment or newness of life." Perhaps a book of synonyms may give a wider margin to the word; but Carpenter's Work furnishes no more than these: "penitence," "contrition," "remorse," "compunction." Perhaps Roget's Thesaurus—in which all the words, whether synonymous or not, that can be gathered under certain generic ideas, are to be found classified—may enlarge the scope of the word in its popular acceptation. But we find it under the head (that is under the *idea* of) "Penitence," and in this company: "contrition," "compunction," "regret," "remorse," "self-reproach," "self-reproof," "self-accusation," "self-condemnation," "qualms or prickings of conscience," "confession," "acknowledgment," "apology," and at the end of the list, as if the last and least association of all—the most remote cousin of all that kindred—"to reclaim, to turn from sin."

It may be said that the word is technical, and that to those properly instructed, it has an additional and peculiar force. But certainly the Bible ought to have no technical terms, or words of arbitrary signification, unless the poverty of the English compels the absolute appropriation of a word to a particular meaning. In view, however, of a possible technical use we turn to the books of theological definitions. Cruden, in his Concordance (a book which accompanies the Bible in many households), thus defines Repentance—"That regret and reluctance that arises in a person after having done something that he ought not to have done"—and the case in point that is cited is the emotion of Judas after he had betrayed his Master. In the technical definition which follows of "Evangelical repentance," it is assigned to "grief" on account of sin, and this feeling "*accompanied by a resolution* to forsake sin, and an expectation of forgiveness." Now to Buck's Theological Dictionary (intended for popular use) : "In general, it is sorrow for anything past. In theology it signifies that sorrow for sin which produces newness of life." In both of these, whether popular or technical, we see "sorrow" represented as the first and almost exhaustive element of the word; in one, amendment of life is implied as a possible consequence of it, while in the other it is mentioned as the result of it. But enough has been quoted to show that the word refers more to emotion than to thought or action, and that *this* is very nearly the exclusive impression conveyed by it.

Now shut the English and open the Greek

Testament. We find John the Baptist and Jesus proclaiming μετανοεῖτε, *metanoeite,* and John proclaiming the "baptism μετανοιας, *metanoias.*" But let us pause a moment here, and go to the word used to express the feeling of Judas after the betrayal, which is also rendered "repent," and which Cruden cites as the primary illustration of the idea. We find μεταμεληθείς, *metameletheis*—a different word. This is only one instance out of many where a single English word is made to do duty for two, not synonymous—nay, in this instance, almost opposite Greek words. But the citation of this alone will serve to show that the "habit" of the A. V. prevents the English reader from making any distinction between the grand call of the Gospel into the way that leadeth unto Life, and the wretched emotion of Judas which led *him* to hang himself. Throughout the A. V. "repent" is indifferently the rendering of either. Thus we have another element of confusion added, and this by the Version itself.

But to return to our word of splendid significance, μετάνοια, *metanoia*. It is compounded of μετα, *meta—after*; and νοέω, *noeô—to perceive*. As the familiar word metamorphosis, from μετα, *meta—after*, and μορφόω, *morphoô—to form*, means a transformation, and in this sense is applied to the changed appearance of our Saviour on the mount, so μετάνοια, *metanoia*, is a " transmentation," to use a coinage of Coleridge—*a change of mind, a change of perception*. The Lexicons of the New Testament define it thus; that of Green: μετανοέω, *metanôeô*, "*to undergo a change in frame of mind and feeling —to make a change of principle and practice, to reform,* * * *practical* reformation—reversal *of the past;*" that of Robinson: "*to perceive afterwards, to have an after-view, hence to change one's views, mind, purpose.*" And he adds, " In a religious sense *implying* sorrow for unbelief and sin, and the turning from them." The *implication* is of sorrow on the one hand, and of turning on the other; but the middle and essential meaning is a *change of perception, or transformation of mind.* From this trunk

14

these two main branches spring, as far as definition is concerned. So much for the word in itself.

But now see the reflexive force of its *circumstances*, keeping it in that signification and sublimating it. Μετανοεῖτε, "*Metanoeite!*" said both John and Jesus, "for the Kingdom of Heaven is at hand!" Μετανοεῖτε, "*Metanoeite!* and believe the good tidings!" The people were summoned to a frame of mind and heart corresponding to this new order of things. The call was not "The wrath of God has come! Repent ye!"—*i. e.* be penitent; but the "Good News has come, the long-expected kingdom has come—prepare yourselves for it. The long-desired Deliverer has come—go ye out to meet Him!" Of course, under the stern, legal preaching of the Baptist that "inward change" sometimes pointed to the "wrath to come," and doubtless that dark side of the bright Gospel was often urged; but what do we find, even in *his* teaching, follows the call to μετάνοια, *metanoia?* Do we read of cries, and tears, and remorse? or is it not just the other way? Is it not action that we see, and only emotion by implication? Stirred by his "exhortations," and his portrayal of the Great One who was at hand, they crowded to his baptism, and going down into the water, "buried" the "old man" in that grave, and rose again as the "new man." If that expressive act was not a vivid symbol of an absolute change, what could be? But still further, see the word in the reflexive light of his *teachings* also—First, as a change of *perception*, νους, *nous*, "Think not," said he to the Pharisees and Sadducees, and (according to Luke) to the multitude as well, "Think not to say within yourselves 'we have Abraham to our father,' for God is able of these stones to raise up children unto Abraham!" A full exposition of *that* statement must have had an enlightening and revolutionizing effect on the minds of those who listened to it; and John, emerging from his ascetic seclusion, in the hairy dress and leathern girdle of an ancient prophet, with the look of Elijah and the voice of Isaiah, was an unquestioned authority on that subject to the multitude, if not always to their leaders. So again, when he said that the axe was laid at the root of the trees, and every tree that brought not forth *good* fruit was to be hewn down, there was material for " reflection" and change of " perception," bordering close on a change of *disposition* also; for the heart is not far off from the mind, and a change of situation in one is apt to induce a change of situation in the other.

And Second, " Bring forth," said he, "fruits worthy of μετάνοια, *metanoia*," and in a few lines we have a digest of his practical teachings of what a man should do, whose perceptions had been changed. Read the μετάνοια, *metanoia*, in this light: To the people who asked " What must we *do*, then?" he said, "He that hath two coats, let him impart to him that hath none; and he that hath meat, let him do likewise." To the publicans, " Exact no more than that which is appointed you." To the soldiers, " Do violence to no man; neither accuse any falsely; and be content with your wages." These glimpses into his teaching are his own definition of μετάνοια, *metanoia*. It was nothing less than a change of view as to principle, and a reformation as to heart and life, and, as far as the stress of the record goes, more of *either* than of sorrow, evidently and strongly as that is implied also. So, if we seek the interpretation of the word from its circumstances, and the import of the proclamation from its effect, we find μετάνοια, *metanoia*, to have a meaning immeasurably deeper and grander than the *repentance* of the dictionaries and the vernacular. It meant just what it was prophesied that John should accomplish. He was to "turn the hearts of the fathers to the children, and the disobedient to the wisdom of the just, to make ready" (not make sorry) "a people prepared for the Lord." (Luke i. 16.)

So the Baptist, uttering the spirit of the Law, which was half-way to the Gospel, urged to a mind and life which conformed to it. And afterwards, when he had done his part, Christ took up the self-same word and theme μετανοεῖτε, *metanoeite!* and carried it on into the full Gospel. The last note of the law, by the last of the prophets, was even what its first note was. "Reform!" live up to the law—leave the wrong—live to the right! And when the Gospel took up its sublime movement, its trumpet rang the self-same note again, and, this time, so that all humanity should hear it —"Reform!" The idea and purpose of the one were only more magnificently the idea and purpose of the other—righteousness of life, genuineness of nature, *faithful and practical morality* of heart and conduct.

Read μετανοεῖτε, *metanoeite*, as proclaimed by the lips of Jesus in the light of *His* teaching also; and see again the infinitely practical significance of the word. Read in it the whole Sermon on the Mount, in which the law was not destroyed, but fulfilled. Read in it every precept and every parable pointing to the Christian life, uttered in the teaching of the long three years to come! The whole weight of that vast morality is thrown into the scale. Which way, then, does the beam turn? towards the emotion on this side of the "changed mind," or towards the action on the other? So great is the preponderance of the latter, that we are more than ever impatient of a word which keeps the fact and its telling, captivating lesson from the people.

And with all this so patent, comes the strangest aspect of this matter. No commentary within my reach notices regretfully this inversion of meaning; hardly any notice it at all—and no one of them suggests the necessity of remedying it. Dean Alford, whose elaborate Greek Testament is so full of fine renderings, and the development, sometimes, of the almost incommunicable force and subtle distinctions of the original, who has issued three different works containing suggestions as to a revision of the A. V., never even pauses at the word, μετανοεῖτε, *metanoeite*, but leaves the "Repent ye," we are so familiar with, to go on uttering its vague, uncertain sound. I turn to a score or more of versions that are lying around me, and can cite but two or three, among them all, that make or suggest an alteration. These exceptions, and eminent ones they are, will be mentioned further on. I open Archbishop Trench's work on the "Synonyms of the Greek New Testament," where so many admirable discriminations appear, and μετανοέω, *metanoeō* and μεταμέλομαι, *metamelomai* are not on the list; at the end of the book, however, in a brief supplementary mention, they are inserted, and reference is made to a Latin extract from Bengel, in the appendix.* But this extract is upon a

---

* A new edition, issued since the above was written, contains a learned and elaborate statement of the question, and in entire agreement with the view now presented. "Μετανοεῖν," he says, "is properly to know *after*, as προνοεῖν to know *before*, and μετάνοια *after*-knowledge, as πρόνοια *fore*-knowledge * * * At its next step μετάνοια signifies the change of mind consequent on this after-knowledge * * * At its third, it is regret for the course pursued; resulting from the change of mind consequent on this after-knowledge * * * Last of all it signifies change of conduct for the future, springing from all this."

passage, in 2 Cor. vii. 8, which I was just about to cite as a culminating instance of confusion and misconception in the A. V. in this regard.

He goes on to say: "At the same time this change of mind, and of action, may be quite as well a change for the worse as for the better; there is no need that it should be a 'rescipiscentia' as well; this is quite a Christian superaddition to the word." Certainly. The word is best defined by its connection—the nature of the change by its circumstances,—a set of bad influences and ideas coming upon a good mind and a good life may produce the μετάνοια, a change of view, disposition, and action.

But Archbishop Trench proceeds: "It is only after μετάνοια has been taken up into the uses of Scripture * * * that it comes predominantly to mean a change of mind, taking a *wiser* view of the past, a regret for the ill-done in that past, and out of all this a change of life for the better * * * in the New Testament μετανοεῖν and μετάνοια are never used in other than an *ethical* sense. * * * But while they gradually advanced in depth and fulness of meaning (he is alluding to a less definite classical use), till they became the fixed and recognised words to express that mighty change in mind, heart, and life wrought by the spirit of God which we call repentance, the like honor was very partially vouchsafed to μεταμέλεια and μεταμέλεσθαι."— *New Testament Synonyms*, p. 241, § lxix.

The two words come together, and no wonder that some one thought it high time to disentangle them from each other—" For though I made you sorry with a letter, I do not *repent* μεταμέλομαι (*metamelomai*, regret), though I did *repent* μεταμελόμην (*metamelomēn*, regret). * * Now I rejoice, not that ye were made sorry, but that ye sorrowed to *repentance* μετάνοιαν (*metanoian*, reformation). For godly sorrow worketh *repentance* μετάνοιαν (*metanoian*, reformation) unto salvation, not to be *repented of* ἀμεταμέλητον (*ametamelēton*, regretted).

The distinction between these two words was evidently thought too small, by the translators, to be of practical account. Their own inadequate perception of the chief one allowed them to admit this play on words, without any thought that it was losing its individual force or significance. And as it is here, so it was allowed to be throughout the New Testament, to the unhappy production of the same confusion of meaning.

It is time, now, in order that the distinction

may be more than ever manifest, to find out exactly what this other word, rendered "repentance," μεταμἑλεια, *metameleia,* means. It is compounded of μετα, *meta,* after, and μελω, *melō*, signifying "care, concern;" μετα, *meta,* gives this "care" or "concern," an *after* character. Concern for an event "to come" is anxiety, but concern for an event "past" would be sorrow. Μεταμἑλεια, *metameleia,* therefore, signifies a *change of care,* a returning to the past with regret. From this, very naturally, proceeds the occasional meaning of a change of one's judgment on past points of conduct, and it mounts into a mental process, which may have a purpose in it, and, so far, a *mind*—but a very different mind from the νους, *nous.* Where is the identity, then, with μετάνοια, *metanoia?* They occupy two different spheres. One acts forward, the other backward. One, μετάνοια, *metanoia,* is a forward movement of view and disposition, which may have part of its occasion in a backward look at its conduct, and regret therefor, but may also be induced by a front occasion of enlightenment and persuasion. The other, μεταμέλεια, *metameleia*, is a backward movement of care, which finds its total existence in the regretted thing done, and has but little forward movement, intelligence and fixedness of purpose. When it has that, it becomes the other, and must change its name. The words diverge as much in their use and application as the English words "remorse" and "reformation." Bengel, in the extract above referred to, draws the distinction thus: "μετάνοια, *metanoia*, belongs properly to the understanding; μεταμέλεια, *metameleia*, to the will; because the former expresses the change of sentiment, the latter the change of care, or rather of purpose. * * * * Μεταμέλεια, *metameleia*, is generally an intermediate term and chiefly refers to single actions; but μετάνοια, *metanoia*, especially in the New Testament, is taken in a good sense, denoting the repentance which concerns the whole life, and, in some respects, ourselves, or that whole blessed remembrance of the mind, after which suitable fruits follow.

Hence it happens that μετάνοειν, *metanoein*, is often put in the imperative; μεταμέλεσθαι, *metamelesthai*, never; but elsewhere, wherever μετάνοια, *metanoia* is read, μεταμέλεια, *metameleia*, may be substituted, but not *vice versâ*."*

Bengel's distinction is made on a review which takes in the use of the words in the *Septuagint*, which is more indiscriminate than the use in the New Testament; both words being put indifferently for one Hebrew word. But a version made in Egypt, in the time of the Ptolemies, three hundred years before the Christian era, cannot be perfect authority for a usage which may have obtained a whole generation after the Christian era. As Campbell says, "we know that in a much shorter period than that which intervened between the translation of the Old Testament, and the composition of the New, some words may become obsolete, and others considerably alter in signification." And he points to the A. V. as an instance of it, where (150 years in

---

* Gnomon on 2 Cor. vii. 10.

his time, in ours 250 years), several words are antiquated, and others bear a different meaning now from what they did then.*

We may dismiss the *Septuagint* then from the discussion of the New Testament usage of these words, especially because, to quote the authority of Campbell again (and the quotation will save a citation of passages), "where this change of mind is inculcated as a *duty*, or the necessity of it mentioned as a doctrine of Christianity, the terms are invariably μετανοεω, *metanoeô*, and μετάνοια, *metanoia*. But when such sorrow is alluded to, as either is not productive of reformation, or, in the nature of the thing, does not imply it, they are never used."†

But, to return to the distinction between them: Wm. Webster, in his "Syntax and Synonyms of the Greek Testament," thus draws the line of difference: "Μεταμέλομαι, *metamelomai*, alter one's purpose, denoting change of feeling, the anxiety consequent on

---

* "Gospels," I. 206, 207.
† Ib. 207, 208.

a past transaction, remorse, sometimes implying a return to a right state of mind, *poenitet, piget*. Μετάνοεω, *metanoeô*, change one's views for the better, implying the sorrow by which sin is forsaken; Latin *resipisco*, recover one's senses, come to a right understanding. Μετάνοια, *metanoia*, conversion, the sanctified effect of μεταμέλεια, *metameleia*, or godly sorrow; *Resipiscentia*, the growing wise. Dr. Wordsworth thus expresses the difference: Μετάνοια, *metanoia*, change of mind, belongs only to the good; μεταμέλεια, *metameleia*, pain of mind, belongs to evil men, as well as good. Peter μετανοεῖ, *metanoei*, as well as μεταμέλεται, *metameletai*. Μετάνοεω, *metanoeô*, begins with μεταμέλεια, *metameleia*, but at length delivers from μεταμέλεια, *metameleia*, whereas μεταμέλεια, *metameleia*, without μετάνοια, *metanoia*, continues to eternity."* I believe there is perfect coincidence and accordance in these extracts with the views set forth above. And when such weighty authorities as these can be cited, what can be

* Syntax and Synonyms of the New Testament, 221–2.

the reason of the silence in other quarters on the subject?

But how did the word "repentance," for μετάνοια, *metanoia*, get into our version? Simply from the influence of the Vulgate and other Latin versions. To this influence not a few expressions in the A. V. can be traced. The Latin was almost vernacular to scholars at that time, and it was as natural to them to refer to a usage in that tongue, as to one in the English. The Vulgate has for μετανοεῖτε, *metanoeite, poenitentiam agite*, which in the Douay-Rheims Bible is rendered "do penance," and which, a footnote says, "does not only signify repentance, and amendment of life, but also punishing past sins by fasting and such like penitential exercises." This idea of "punishment" comes from *poena* the root of the word. Out of "penance" comes "penitent," "one who is penitent or sorrowful for sin; a repentant" (Worcester); and "penitence" is "the state of being penitent." In the Vulgate, there is no discrimination between μετάνοια, *metanoia*, and μεταμέλεια, *metameleia*, as we might well suppose. The English word has thus become saturated with the idea of "pain," "penalty," and never suggests, except by implication, the idea of change or reformation.

Beza, in his Latin version, in a true Protestant spirit, went back to the fountain head, and, in trying to render the Greek more exactly, introduced the word *resipisco* for μετάνοεω, *metanoeô*, and *resipiscentia* for μετάνοια, *metanoia*. In this the surcharging influence of "penitence," "pain," suggested by the Vulgate, was eliminated and the idea of the Greek word was more nearly approached. Beza would seem to have derived μετανοια, *metanoia*, from μετα, *meta*, and ανοια, *anoia* ; ανοια, *anoia*, want of understanding, folly, rashness, heedlessness; a change, therefore, from a want of mind, or perception, a return to one's senses. This, Adam Clark seems also to prefer.* *Resipisco* (from *re* and *sapere*) conveys the idea of a "return to wisdom," and might be made to mean all that

---

* Cf. Comm. in loc.

is conveyed by μετάνοεω, *metanoeô*. It was a decided divergence from the Vulgate, and drew Beza into controversy with the Roman Catholic theologians who preferred *poenitentia* to *resipiscentia* because, to quote Archbishop Trench, "hallowed by long ecclesiastical usage, and having acquired a certain prescriptive right, by its long employment in the Vulgate."* I suppose a change of "repentance" to some word more expressive, would be resisted now in some quarters on the same grounds. But Beza could cite ancient ecclesiastical authority for the change. With the decided influence which his Version had upon Protestant theologians, his Greek text too being the chief reliance of those who formed the A. V., it seems strange that the equivalent at least of *resipisco* was not put into English. *Repent* does not represent it, neither "mind" nor "want of mind," are suggested by it, but it would seem to be a sort of mild rendering of the Vulgate, at any rate betraying its influence in keeping uppermost the

* Authorized Version, 52.

idea of penitence. Repentance, was certainly never born of μετανοια, *metanoia*, which Beza always renders by *resipiscentia*.

"*Poenitentia* is at fault," says Trench, "in that it brings out nothing but a serious displeasure on the sinner's part at his past life, and leaves the changed mind for the time to come, which is the central idea of the original word, altogether unexpressed and untouched."* And yet Trench resists the alteration! What then is the force of *re-poenitentia?* Nothing more, it seems to me, than "repentance" in its ordinary and popular acceptation.

But in alluding to the Vulgate, and its authority for such a strange inversion and suppression (perhaps want of development) of the meaning of μετανοεῖτε, *metanoeite*, we have another and even older index of the ancient meaning. The Syriac Version,—the oldest known to scholars, written in the very language spoken by the Baptist, by the Saviour, and by the people; a rendering back from the Greek

* " Authorized Version," 52.

into the Aramaic, and not unlikely, in this instance, into the very words originally spoken, is uniform in preserving the distinction between Reformation and Repentance. Μετάνοειν, *melanoein*, it renders (see Campbell) *thub*, "to reform, to return to God, to amend one's life;" μετάνοια, *metanoia*, *thebutha*, a "reformation;" μεταμελεσθαι, *metamelesthai*, is rendered *thua* "to repent," "to be sorry for what one has done.*

Nothing could be more satisfactory, after an analysis of the Greek words themselves, than this almost vernacular evidence of their primitive meaning. The two languages, one born on the spot, and the other occupying the country; one the speech of its people, the other the dialect of their Scriptures—unite most impressively here to condemn the Latin intrusion. It rouses in us something of the spirit of that ancient people to be rid of the Roman yoke, and to possess our heritage free of such alien repression.

After all this, we may be allowed to wonder

* "Gospels" 211.

at the indifference of theologians to such an important distinction—a distinction which, if made, would amount almost to a revelation to the people. The practical effect of the word "repentance" when representing μετάνοια, *metanoia*, in the New Testament, is to give a foremost consequence to "penitence," and to keep its possible, but all requisite result, "amendment," in the background. *The tendency of the popular mind is to lose sight of the fact that the first design of the Gospel is to produce reformation of heart and life;* and this unfortunate rendering has done *not a little to form that general misapprehension as to the end and aim of the Christian religion, and to encourage that mere emotionalism, in which so much of the Christian impulse is content to remain.* And is it not *occasion enough for regret, and for discussion too, when it can be truly said of this rendering that, from the initial position, and foreshadowing character of the word, it affects the distinctness of the moral system of the New Testament, and does not adequately suggest the ethical character of the Christian Religion.* But give μετάνοια, *metanoia,* its full intrinsic force, and then we have identically that divine change which John, in the beginning of his Gospel, with such characteristic memory and insight, reports as the early call of Jesus: "Ye must be born again." Now all four Gospels become strikingly and vividly accordant at once. They all utter the same note. Remark the correspondence: the Baptist, in Mark and Luke, preaching "the Baptism of Reformation." JESUS, in Matthew, "Reform! for the kingdom of heaven is at hand!" In Mark—"The time is fulfilled, and the kingdom of God has come, Reform!" In John—"Except a man be born again he cannot see the kingdom of God!" In Matthew—"Except be ye converted (*i. e.* changed into something else) and become as little children, ye shall not enter the kingdom of heaven." Nor does it stop here. Peter, in the Acts, cries "Reform! and be baptized every one of you for the remission of sins." "Reform (become changed in mind), therefore, and be *converted* (changed in life), that your sins may be blotted out." Paul, in Corinthians, writes, " If any man be in Christ he is a new creature, old things are passed away, behold all things are become new," and in Ephesians—" Be renewed in the spirit of your mind—put on the new man."

Thus the whole system seems to have been grasped in the long reach of its first great heralding word, and becomes from beginning to end sublimely consistent with itself.

But admitting the inadequacy of this rendering, as many may be ready to do, the question will rise *how* to change it. It is not a question whether it shall be changed at all, as one might be led to ask in view of the probable objections of those who would cling to it as it is, despite its error, solely on the ground of its long use and hallowed association—the Roman Catholic reason, as we have seen above, against the Bezan departure from the Vulgate; but *how* can it be changed or remedied? The word "Repentance" takes its inadequate force into the whole literature of Christianity. It pervades Catechisms, and established formularies of doctrine, and even the Prayer Book itself. If this difficulty did not exist, the suggestion of Dr. Campbell and more lately of Mr. Robert Young, might be adopted.* They prefer the words "Reform," "Reformation," for the μετανοια, *metanoia*, leaving "Repent" and "Repentance" to stand, where they represent the idea of the μετα, *meta*, and μελω, *melô*. "*Imagine our New Testament opening with the clarion call " Reform !" and the whole working of the Gospel untechnically declared to be from Baptism on, as unto " Reformation," and what a new association and vivid interest would be awakened ! how much more grandly, too, would the historic event and spectacle of the Glad Tidings appear !*"

That noble Version, "the Genevan," of whose singular independence and wisdom I

---

* Campbell, Gospels, I. 207. "The Holy Bible translated according to the Letter and Idioms of the Original Languages," by Robert Young, Edinburgh, in loc.

have had occasion to speak so frequently in the preceding pages, renders "*Amend your lives*" for "Repent ye." The rendering is in three words, instead of one, but with exactly the same meaning.* As a single word is the more desirable, "Reform" would seem on the whole, to be the best English equivalent for μετανοεῖτε, *metanoeite*, for, if it leans at all, it leans *forward* to action, and not backward to sorrow, as "Repentance" certainly does. No one word in our language can exactly represent the significant original, and therefore, the nearest that can be found ought to be used, and then a glossarial foot-note assign and limit it to the full philological force of the Greek. The word "Reform" carries with it much of that massiveness and definiteness of meaning which belonged to the original word that ushered in the Gospel. As defined by Worcester, it means "To change

---

* In Matt. iii. 8. "Bring forth therefore fruits *meet for repentance*," the marginal rendering is, "*answerable to amendment of life.*" Why is this glimpse of the true meaning given here and no hint of it repeated elsewhere?

from worse to better;" "to correct;" "to amend;" "to restore;" "to reclaim" (not one allusion to "repent," by the way). We use the word of individuals when they have turned from some especial course of wickedness. Any public sentiment which looks to the correction of evils, or to social improvement, or to a change for the better in humanity, is known by this significant name. We apply it to the great change for the better in the Church three hundred years ago. And as it seems to me, when we consider the *national* and revolutionary significance of the Baptist's call and its *individual* application and reception together, we could not find a word so instantly and completely equivalent as this. In any future Version which can insulate itself from theologies and systems, and which shall seek to give only the independent force of the original, this without question ought to be the rendering of μετάνοια, *metanoia*.

For the present, and until some such radical alteration be demanded and listened to, it ought to be possible to reverse entirely the present meaning of the word *Repentance*, to give it arbitrarily the exact force of μετάνοια, *metanoia*, and of reformation, and to drop out of it, as much as can be, its old and foremost meaning. Let it become absolutely and confessedly technical—objectionable as that would be—and hereafter enter the dictionaries as such; be defined when theologically used, as "reform," "change of mind, of character, of conduct, of life," and be made generally synonymous with "reform." And, perhaps, also the smaller and easier change of μεταμέλεια, *metameleia*, into "regret" (if such should happily come in a new "Authorized Version)," may leave it to utter with less confusion its grander meaning.

T. W.

THE END.